Dinah Zike's
Big Book of
Holiday Activities

By Dinah Zike, M.Ed.

dma

dinah-might activities

Other books and videos by Dinah Zike:

The Big Book of Books and Activities
The Big Book of Projects
Great Tables, Graphs, Charts, Diagrams, and Timelines You Can Make!
Science Poems, Riddles, and Rhymes: Earth, Solar System, and Universe
Science Poems, Riddles, and Rhymes: Land, Water, Air, and Weather
The Earth Science Book
Video: How to Use the Big Book of Books
Video: How to Use the Big Book of Projects
Time Twister Chronicles: The Search For T. Rex
Time Twister Chronicles: Rainforest Rescue

Dinah's books are available in teacher bookstores or can be ordered from:

Dinah-Might Activities, Inc.
P.O. Box 690328
San Antonio, Texas, 78269
Office: (210) 698-0123
Fax: (210) 698-0095
Orders: 1-800-99-DINAH (993-4624)

Introduction

Welcome to the *Big Book of Holiday Activities*. It is the third in my series of *Big Books*, and it is a collection of some of my favorite holiday craft projects and writing activities for the classroom and home. The manipulatives in this book are based upon the folds introduced in my award winning *Big Book of Books and Activities*, and *The Big Book of Projects*.

I have spent over 15 years conducting seminars and staff development workshops across the United States, sharing the folds that I've invented or adapted to make academic graphic organizers. During my workshops, as an aside, I quickly include holiday uses for the folds that I am in the process of illustrating for multidisciplinary student activities and assessment. Through the years I have received hundreds of requests to put all of my holiday ideas into one big book. Well, its been years in the making, but it is finally ready.

Happy Holidays and Enjoy,

Dinah Zike, M.Ed.

Table of Contents

Table of Contents

Important Message

I DO NOT encourage the use of duplicated materials in the classroom. I am noted for inventing books and manipulatives to take the place of ditto sheets and workbook pages. I feel it is important for students to be responsible for their own work, and that includes writing 8 to 15 times a day. I see too many students who want to fill in blanks instead of writing on their own. I am also opposed to giving too many coloring sheets to students. However, I do not feel it is wrong to give a student a template or stencil to use creatively.

The majority of the patterns included in the back of this book are to be used by the teacher (and students) to make classroom sets of templates for students to trace around. Some patterns have illustrations on them. These patterns can be used three ways: they can be photocopied for each student; students can trace over the illustration on the front of the templates; or they can draw their own details on the template outlines. Allow students total artistic freedom. Many will want to design their own templates as they learn how they are used.

We have made each of these template patterns a specific size to fit on the folds featured in this book. Tracing over and around patterns, pictures, and templates is good for enhancing fine motor skills and coordination; plus, each student has more time and creativity invested in the project, resulting in a sense of ownership and pride.

Template-Pattern Activities: garlands, milk carton boxes, ornaments, picture frame books, trifold books, display box lids, layered look books, and match books.

Photocopied or Student Traced Activities: cubes, banners, shutterfolds, accordions, large table displays, large ornaments, and holiday cereal boxes.

How to Make Posterboard Templates

1. Select and photocopy a holiday season pattern.

2. Cut along the solid black lines of the photocopy.

3. Trace around the pattern onto
   a piece of heavy poster board.

4. Cut out the traced posterboard shapes, and make
   them available to students in your classroom
   publishing center.

5. Students place the posterboard template onto a
   folded paper activity, trace around it, then cut it out.

6. Store templates in baggies, file them away,
   and they will be ready for use year after year.

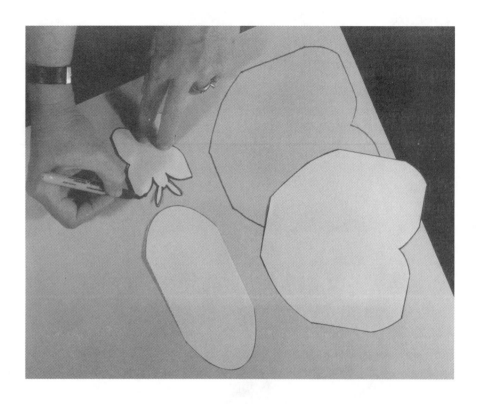

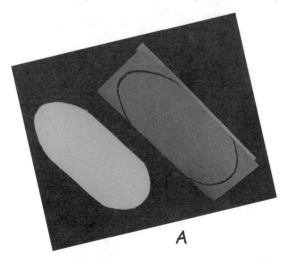

A

B

The light colored object in picture "A"
is a posterboard template of an egg.
A student traced around this template
on a trifold book. When cut out, as in
picture "B," an egg-shaped trifold book is
ready for writing activities.

How to Make Posterboard Templates

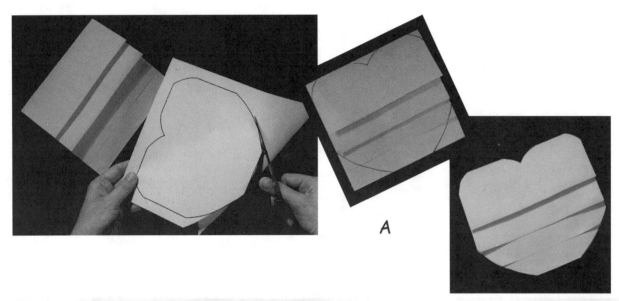

A

A. Layered Look Book using a template.

B. Accordion Book and/or Garland using a template.

C. Desk Top Project using a template.

B

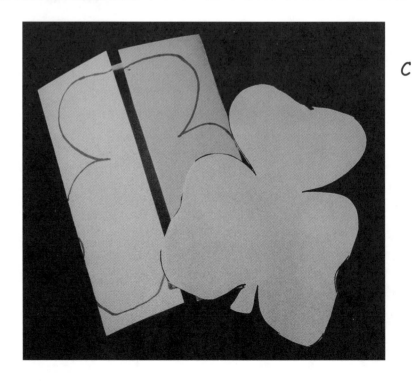

C

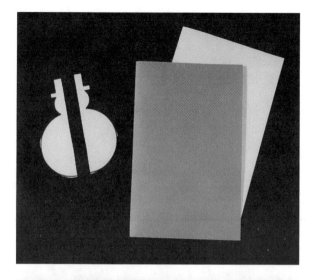

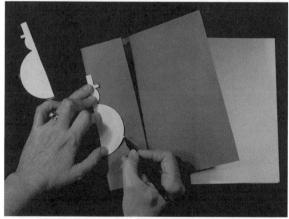

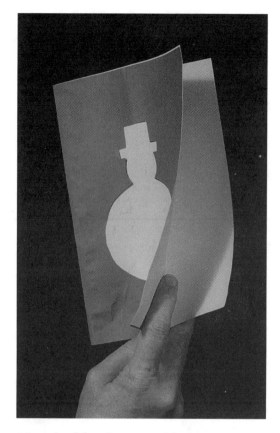

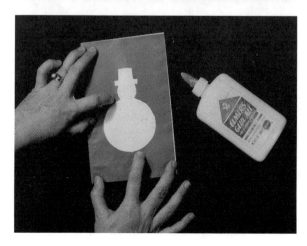

Use half of a template pattern to cut a symmetrical shape on a folded piece of paper as illustrated in the photos of this pictureframe book.

Small Patterns Can be Used to Make:
- Small garlands
- Small ornaments
- Wreaths
- Milk carton boxes
- Lids for display boxes

Medium Patterns Can be Used to Make:
- Picture frame books
- Large ornaments

Large Patterns Can be Used to Make:
- Layered look books
- Backing for matchbooks

Full-Page Patterns Can be Used to Make:
- Shutterfolds
- Cereal box covers
- Large accordion books
- Display cubes
- Giant ornaments

Trifold Patterns Can be Used to Make:
- Trifold books
- Large garlands

Decorate With:
- Crayons, markers, or colored pencils
- Paints or pastels
- Stickers or stamps
- Glitter or beads
- Decorative hole punches
- Greeting cards, wrapping paper, torn paper, etc.

Holiday Story Starters

This is how I...
I couldn't believe it when...
I wish I had...
I am thankful for...
I love or like...
I am excited to get to...
My favorite holiday smells...
Things I hear people say this time of the year...
I enjoyed making _____ for this holiday...
I (am or am not) glad this holiday comes only once a year. Why?
During this holiday, time seems to...
When I think of this holiday I think of...
Compare and contrast this holiday to one similar to it in another country...
Not every country celebrates this holiday because...
These are the steps to... (Bake a birthday cake, wrap a present, etc.)
Effect of the holiday on my daily life?
Effect of the holiday on my community? Nation?
Who, what, when, and where or why of the holiday season...
What, where, when and how of the holiday season...
This holiday makes me feel...
During this holiday I usually wear...
I like the weather to be _____ during this holiday...
At _____ o'clock we did... or we will...
Compare and contrast homemade decorations and store bought ones...
(How do they look? How do they make you feel? Which have the most meaning?)

Holiday Story Starters

What color or colors represent this season and why?
This is the geometric shape I think of when I think of this holiday... Why?
I feel this holiday comes (quickly or slowly) each year...
Three things I will remember about this holiday...
Family traditions that are important to me...
Something I would make into a tradition...
Food and More Food: My holiday food diary...
Dairy of a Holiday Sweet Tooth...
Holiday Recipe Book: How to cook my favorite holiday sweets...
History of this Holiday: Library or internet research and reporting...
Create your own holiday and explain it in detail...
Describe what the world would be like without any holidays...
Do you think we have enough or not enough holidays? Why?
What would happen if every day were a holiday?
I hope I get to _____this holiday...
I wish I didn't have to _____ this holiday...
Develop a holiday "interview" and record how people respond to your interview questions...
Look at holiday ads and write about the commercialization of the holiday...
Investigate and speculate: A Holiday Past, Present, and Future...
Think of a problem that always arises during this holiday: Problem, Cause, and Effect...
How do you justify the amount of time and/or money you spend on a specific holiday?
Explain the words of a "traditional" holiday song or poem...
Write your own "traditional" holiday song, poem, or story...
If I could use only one decoration it would be...
I could do these things to help others this holiday season...

Holiday Trifold Books

See pages 84-87 of *Dinah Zike's Big Book of Books and Activities*
for fold instructions and academic applications for this book.

1. Make trifold templates out of posterboard.
2. Make a trifold book.
3. Place the trifold template on top of the trifold book and trace around it.
4. Cut around the traced lines. Notice that trifold templates have flat sides
that form hinges. Each book will have three sections as in photograph B.

Use this book to make an advertising brochure for a holiday adventure.
Great for writing activities that come in threes:

   -Beginning, middle, and ending or first, next, and last.
   -Past, present, and future.
   -K-LK-L (What do you know?; What would you like to know?;
         What have you learned?).
   -Problem, cause, and effect.

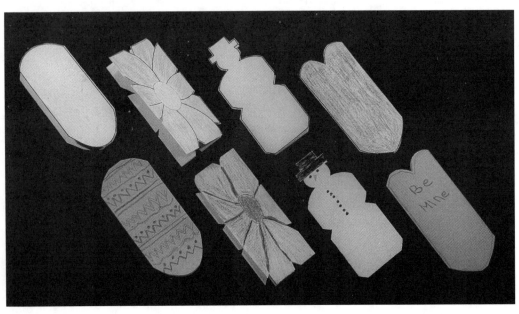 A

 B

Pop-Up Books

See pages 112-115 of *Dinah Zike's Big Book of Books and Activities*
for fold instructions and academic applications for this book.

1. Make a pop-up book.
2. Use the small patterns in this book to make pop-up illustrations for:
   - Holiday or special occasion greeting cards.
   - Party invitations.
   - Sentence or paragraph writing activities.
   - Word lists.
   - Holiday book reports.

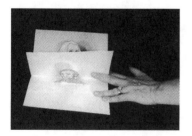

Pop-up books can be made as single-page cards and writing activities or multi-page report books.

Holiday Pop-Up Tree

Pop-out lantern hints:

- Lantern cuts always begin on a fold.

- They are made by a series of cuts at the same or varying lengths.

- The cuts are always shorter than the width of the paper, leaving an uncut area or "tab" around all edges of the paper.

Christmas Tree:

1. Place two sheets of paper together and fold into a hamburger.

2. While folded, cut into the fold every half inch down the length of the fold. The first cut should be the longest, followed by increasingly shorter cut lengths.

3. Trim off excess paper at an angle, leaving a half-inch tab around the cuts.

4. Separate the two sheets of paper and glue them together along the half-inch tab. Fold into a tree shape as shown.

Picture Frame Books

See page 88 of *Dinah Zike's Big Book of Books and Activities*
for fold instructions and academic applications for this book.

1. Make a picture frame book, but instead of making a rectangular frame,
   use **medium**-sized templates and cut them in half. See page 9 for
   symmetrical cutting instructions.
2. Trace around the half pattern.
3. Cut along the trace line.
4. Open the fold to discover a symmetrical cut-out shape framed
   by the rest of the paper.
5. Place glue around the inside edges of the frame and glue to a second
   equal sized sheet of paper.

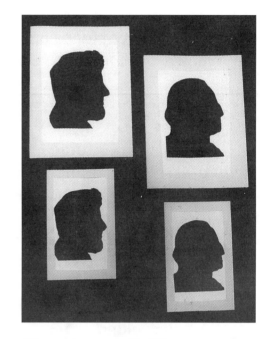

Use this holiday picture
frame book for the
following activities:
- Creative writing
- Research reports
- Autograph books
- Holiday journals
- Biographies
- "me, myself and I"

See p. 9 for symmetrical cutting instructions.

Glue the small silhouettes
featured in this book onto
the front of a picture
frame book.

Layered Look Books

See page 70 of *Dinah Zike's Big Book of Books and Activities*
for fold instructions and academic applications for this book.

1. Using two sheets of paper make a layered look book. Place the sheets of paper about one inch apart before folding and make each tab about one inch in length. Glue together or staple.
2. Cut out the pattern for a layered look book and place it on top of the folded book.
3. Trace around the pattern and cut the folded book into the desired shape.

Use to record holiday events in sequential order:
- First, next, or last
- Beginning, middle, or ending

Use to write or draw about three things:
Example: "December Holiday"
- Where I Will Be
- What I Will See
- What I Will Eat

Use to record steps:
- For making something
- For cooking
- For growing a plant from seeds

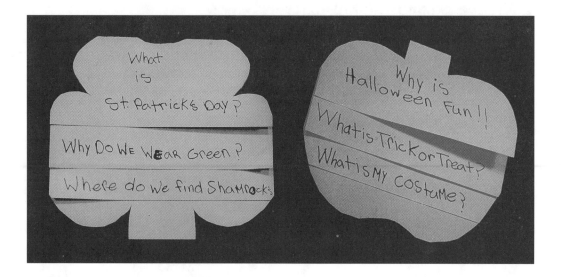

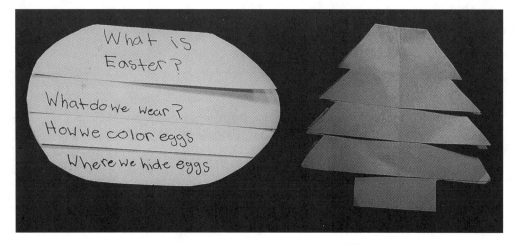

Layered Look Books

See page 70 of *Dinah Zike's Big Book of Books and Activities*
for fold instructions and academic applications for this book.

Describe each of Columbus' ships, its passengers, and cargo. This book can also be used for a research report on the Age of Exploration: Magellan, Balboa, and Colombus. (See p. 127.)

Record what happens on each of the Twelve Days of Christmas.

17

Holiday Match Books

See pages 26-33 of *Dinah Zike's Big Book of Books and Activities*
for fold instructions and academic applications for this book.

1. Fold a match book.
2. Use it for a writing activity. For example: Title on outside and paragraph inside,
     or a question on the outside and an answer inside.
3. Glue it onto a holiday pattern. (The layered-look pattern is a good size for this.)
4. Encourage students to creatively and individually decorate their writing activity
     using a variety of supplies and materials.

Use small matchbooks
to create a calendar.
Write the date on the
front and record an
event or word for that
day under the tab.

Not pictured:
Match books can also
be cut into shapes.
See page 30 of the
*Big Book of Books and
Activities.*

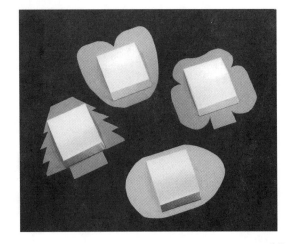

Holiday Boxes

See page 59 of *Dinah Zike's Big Book of Projects*
for fold instructions and academic applications for this book.

1. Make a display case, but do not glue the lid.
2. Make **small** patterns and cut them in half as with the picture frame book (p. 15).
3. Fold the lid in half.
4. Place the cut edge of the pattern along the fold of the paper.
5. Trace around the half pattern.
6. Cut along the trace line.
7. Open the fold to discover a symmetrical shape cut out in the middle of the box lid.
8. Finish making the lid by gluing the sides.
9. Cut a piece of acetate to fit inside the lid. Glue it in to make a see-through top.
(Scraps of laminating film or kitchen plastic wrap can also be used.)

Fill the box with:
 -Homemade potpourri
 -Homemade note paper
 -Homemade candy or treats
 -Student-made miniature cards
 (cutouts of small patterns
 written on front and back)

19

Holiday Banners

1. Photocopy a full-page shutterfold pattern for each student.
2. Color and cut them out.
3. Connect numerous patterns onto one long piece of yarn by taping to their back.
4. Hang the banner across a room or hall.

Uses

Birthday Cake Banner:
- "Happy Birthday " notes from students to another student.
- Write one giant letter on each cake to spell "Happy Birthday".

Book Banner:
- Add a book to the banner each time a classroom book is read.
- Keep track of the books an individual student has read.

Flag Banner:
- Great state (use the blank flag to draw your own) or national holiday activity and decoration.

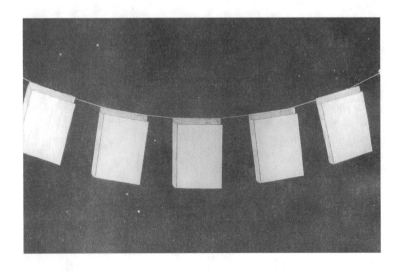

Holiday Desk Top Projects

See page 42 of *Dinah Zike's Big Book of Books and Activities*
for fold instructions and academic applications for this book.

Photocopy Option

1. Make a shutterfold using 11" X 17" paper. This is the size of the largest photocopy paper.
It is inexpensive and thin enough for a young child to fold. Construction paper is hard for children to fold.
2. Run off a copy of the shutterfold pattern of your choice for each student.
Students color the picture, cut it out, fold it in half, cut it in half along the fold line,
and glue it to the two sides of their folded shutterfold.

  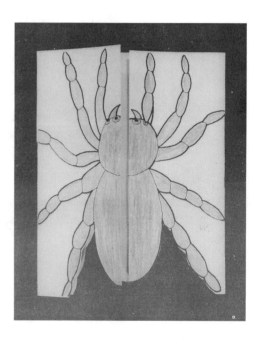

Template Option

1. Photocopy the shutterfold patterns. Glue them to a piece of posterboard. Cut them out to make templates.
2. Make a shutterfold using 11" X 17" paper.
3. Trace around the shutterfold template and cut it out. Students can draw a holiday picture on their
shutterfold while looking at your pattern, or they can place the pattern inside the shutterfold and trace over it!
4. Laminate these templates and they will last for many years.

Desk Top Projects

See page 42 of *Dinah Zike's Big Book of Books and Activities*
for fold instructions and academic applications for this book.

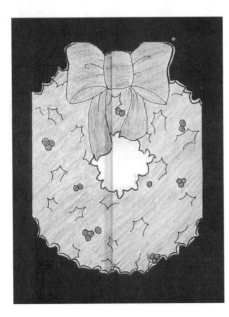

Desk Top Projects

See page 42 of *Dinah Zike's Big Book of Books and Activities*
for fold instructions and academic applications for this book.

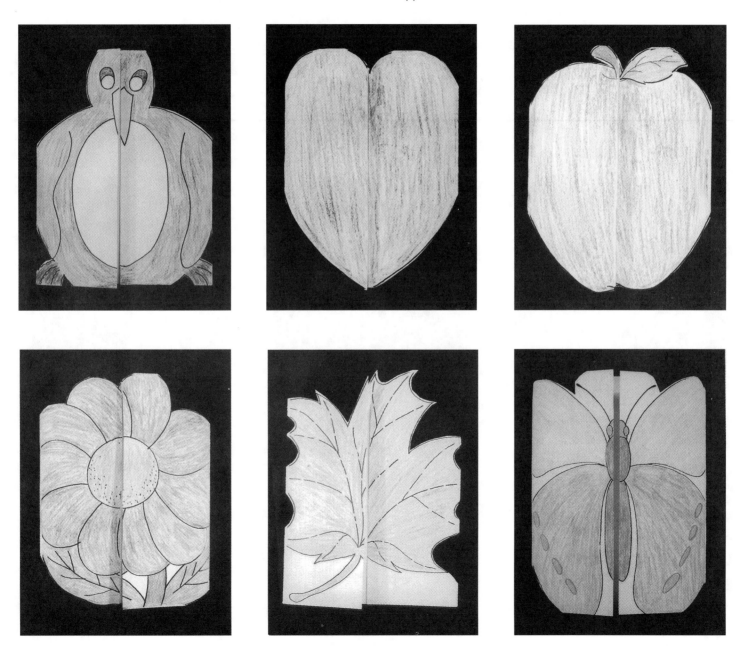

Desk Top Projects

See page 42 of *Dinah Zike's Big Book of Books and Activities*
for fold instructions and academic applications for this book.

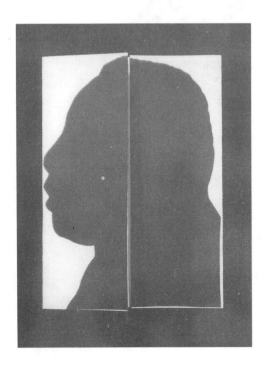
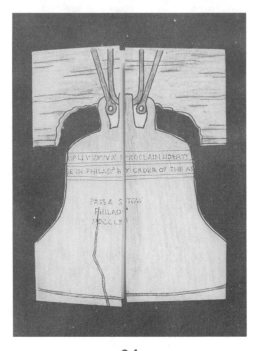

Four-Door Books

See page 44 of *Dinah Zike's Big Book of Projects*
for fold instructions and academic applications for this book.

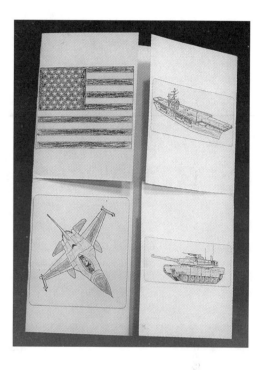

1. Make a shutterfold and fold it in half like a hamburger.
2. Cut both flaps along the hamburger fold to create four doors as shown.
3. Glue or draw pictures on the front of each door, or write a title or question.
4. Write or draw behind each door.

- Use for comparing and contrasting four holiday celebrations in four different countries.
- Use for a holiday book report: Character, plot, setting, and conflict/resolution.

Examples of uses include:
- Earth Day: reduce, reuse, recycle, refuse.
- Armed Forces Day: researching different branches of service.
- Thanksgiving: Native American vs. Pilgrim view of the celebration.

Other Four-door holiday projects:

Who, What, When, and Where

What, Where, When, and Why

What, Where, When, and How

Four-Door Diorama

See page 47 of *Dinah Zike's Big Book of Projects*
for fold instructions and academic applications for this book.

Use large and small four-door dioramas:
-to make 2-dimensional holiday scenes.
-to make holiday pop-up scenes.
-to display holiday books.
-to display holiday ornaments or objects from other countries.
-to compare and contrast a holiday as it is celebrated by different cultures.

Staple dioramas end-to-end to show a sequence of holiday events:
-The Twelve Days of Christmas.
-Events that led up to Cinco de Mayo.
-Events that led up to the first Thanksgiving.
-Events in the life of a historic figure: Dr. Martin Luther King, Abraham Lincoln, etc.

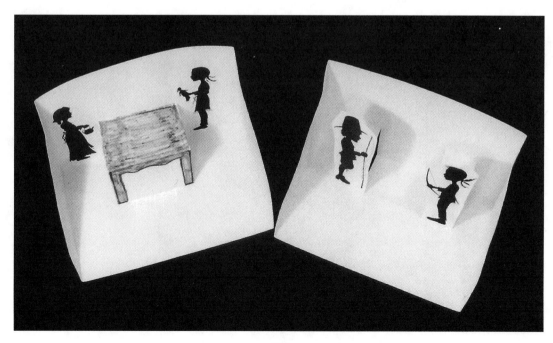

Holiday Cereal Box Covers

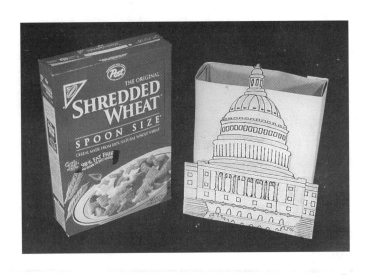

1. Photocopy a full-page shutterfold pattern.
2. Color and cut it out.
3. Glue it to one side of a cereal box with the top cut off.
4. Decorate the other sides using scraps of colored paper, paint, old greeting cards, student drawn art, etc.

Use the boxes for:
- Classroom or individual student holiday mail boxes.
- Taking student-made presents home to family members.
- Storing holiday books.
- Storing holiday writing activities.
- Storing holiday song or poetry sheets.

Accordion Fold Project

See page 57 of *Dinah Zike's Big Book of Projects*
for fold instructions and academic applications for this book.

Use for reports on:
- People born on the months featured.
- Events occuring during the months featured.

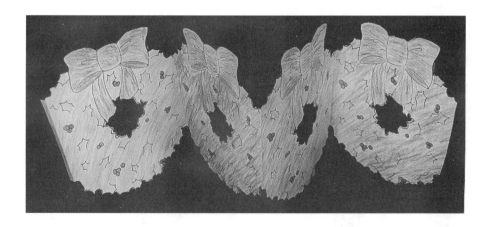

1. Photocopy a full-page shutterfold pattern for each student onto 9" X 12" paper.
   You might have to hand feed this size paper through the copy machine.
2. Have students complete a writing activity on the BACK of the illustration.
3. Color and cut out the picture, but do not cut one of the sides. This will leave a tab along one edge.
4. Fold the tab and glue it behind the next illustration.
5. Glue all student writing projects together along the tabs, forming an accordion fold.

Cube Project

See page 54 of *Dinah Zike's Big Book of Projects*
for fold instructions and academic applications for this book.

1. Photocopy four full-page shutterfold patterns onto 9" X 12" paper.
   You might have to hand feed this size paper through the copy machine.
2. Color and cut out each illustration, but do not cut the right hand side, leaving a tab.
3. Fold back the tab, and glue it to the back of the left side of the second illustration.
4. Glue the second illustration's tab to the left side of the third illustration, and so on
   until you have formed a box or "cube."

Use For: Cafeteria table decorations; signs for table top exhibits; decorate potted plants, jars of pencils or crayons, and open-topped coffee cans used for storage, supplies, and collections.

 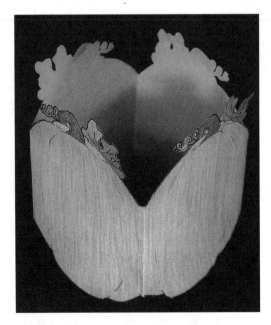 

NOTE: You can also use the medium and small illustrations in this book to make cube projects.

Large Holiday Display
and Ornaments

1. Photocopy four full-page, shutterfold patterns onto 8.5" X 11" paper.
2. Color the pictures and cut them out.
3. Fold all four pictures in half so the colored part does not show.
4. Glue the four folded pictures together on the uncolored side.
5. Fan them around and glue the first and last sections together.

NOTE: For hanging ornaments, glue a string in the middle while doing Step 5.

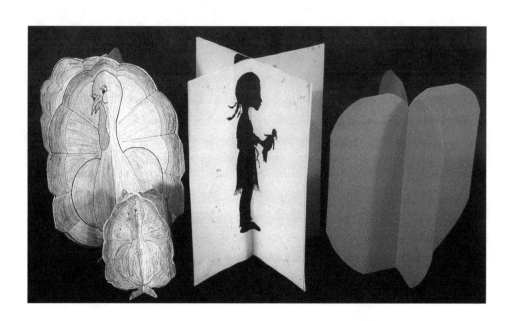

Use For:
- Table Decorations.
- Giant ornaments to hang from the ceiling.
- Displaying four pages of student writing.
- Displaying four pages of student illustrations.

Small 3-D Holiday Ornaments

See pages 64-66 of *Dinah Zike's Big Book of Books and Activities*
for fold instructions and academic applications for this mobile.

1. Cut out four small patterns for each ornament. Decorate these as desired.
2. Fold each in half and glue the half sections together. Fan them around and
     run a piece of yarn through the center.
3. Glue the first and last sections together enclosing the yarn in the center of the 3-D ornament.
4. Allow glue to dry before using ornament.

Uses:
-Hang them from a holiday mobile. (See page 39 of this book.)
-Hang them from a holiday tree. (See page 33 of this book.)
-Run a length of wire instead of yarn through the middle of a series
     of ornaments to make holiday wreaths. (See page 36 of this book.)
-Place pipe cleaners instead of yarn in the middle (photo, right)
     and use them in fresh or dried holiday flower arrangements.

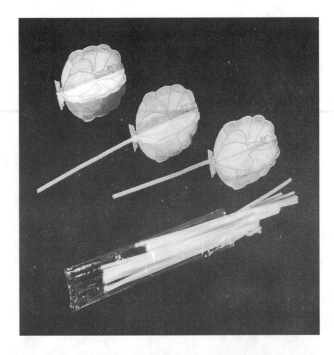

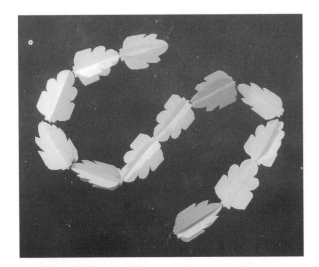

Run a string through the ornaments before gluing them together to form a 3-D garland.

Use the garland on holiday
trees, draped around windows
and doors, or down the center
of a table.

Glue each ornament around a pipe
cleaner and use them in flower
arrangements or make a bouquet of
ornaments.

Small 3-D Holiday Ornaments

See pages 64-66 of *Dinah Zike's Big Book of Books and Activities*
for fold instructions and academic applications for this mobile.

Find a small fallen tree branch. Leave it natural, or
paint it (silver or gold is fun). Place the end into a
large coffee can filled with sand or plaster of Paris.
Wrap the can with butcher paper or giftwrap, and
tie a large bow at the top of the can. You can also
use a cube project (page 30) to decorate the can.

Small Flat Holiday Ornaments

Trace a small template onto foil,
art paper, gift wrap paper, butcher paper,
or any decorative paper.

Two cutout shapes are needed
to form each ornament.

Place a six- to eight-inch piece of
yarn between the shapes so that it
extends several inches above the top
of the ornament.

Glue the shapes back-to-back,
capturing one end of the yarn
between them.

Hang the ornaments by the yarn.

Mixed Small Ornaments & Garland

Use two- and three-dimensional ornaments to decorate holiday trees.
Use garlands on, or under your holiday trees.

Holiday Wreaths

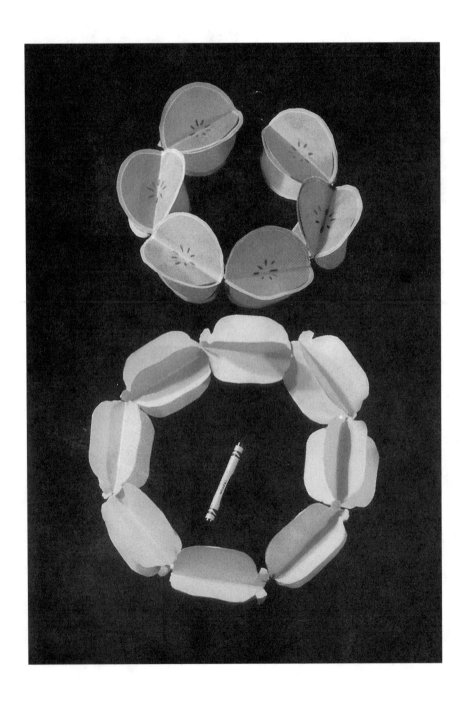

When making three-dimensional ornaments (p.32), run a single length of florist's wire or yarn through the middle of each one before gluing. Make sure the wire or yarn is at least one foot longer than the desired circumference of your holiday wreath.

Once the wreath is the desired size, tie the ends of the wire or yarn together and add a bow, a bell, or other holiday ornaments or decorations.

Hang the wreath on a door, in a window, or suspend it from the ceiling.

Holiday Garlands

See page 102 of *Dinah Zike's Big Book of Books and Activities*
for fold instructions and academic applications for an accordion fold.

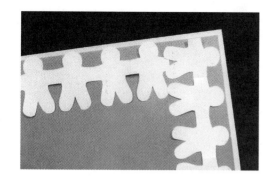

1. Fold an 8 1/2" X 11" sheet of paper into a hot dog fold.
2. Fold the hot dog (a long rectangle) in half like a hamburger.
3. Fold both ends of the hamburger back to touch the mountain top fold.
   (Simply stated, fold the hot dog into an accordion fold.)

4. On one side of the accordion book, trace around a small holiday pattern.
5. The vertical sides of the traced pattern must NOT be cut---the folds along these sides form hinges.
6. The cut will result in two garlands each with four sections.
   Tape or glue garlands edge to edge to reach the desired length.

Pyramids

See page 38 of *Dinah Zike's Big Book of Books and Activities*
for fold instructions and academic applications for this book.

1. Make a pyramid out of a light colored sheet of paper
(white or very light blue to represent sky) and glue it together.
2. Make a pyramid out of dark blue paper and cut it to represent waves.
3. Glue this cut pyramid together and place it over the light-colored pyramid.
4. Use the black-line patterns of the *Nina*, *Pinta*, and *Santa Maria* in the October section of this book.

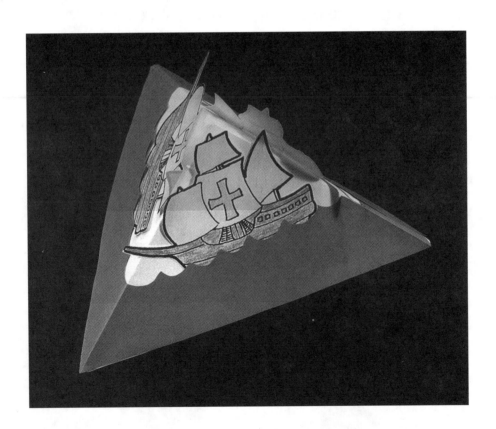

Pyramid Mobile

See page 41 of *Dinah Zike's Big Book of Books and Activities*
for fold instructions and academic applications for this book.

1. Make a pyramid mobile.
2. Snip a tiny hole at the top of the pyramid and push a length of yarn through the
   hole to hang the mobile. Fold a piece of tape or tape a small piece of paper at
   the end of the yarn inside the pyramid to keep it from pulling through the hole.
3. Hang small three-dimensional or flat ornaments (pages 32-35) from the pyramid.

NOTE: Instead of tying knots, allow young children to use cellophane tape
   on the end of the yarn.

Advanced Alternate Activity:
   Make pyramids out of graduated sizes of paper and hang
   them to make a mobile Christmas tree as illustrated (far right).

Pyramid Dioramas

See pages 38-40 of *Dinah Zike's Big Book of Books and Activities*
for fold instructions and academic applications for this project.

1. Make two or four pyramids and glue them together
   to make these dioramas.
2. Use any of the small or medium patterns or illustrations
   to decorate your dioramas.

Use four-pyramid dioramas to illustrate:
- Four events in the life of a historic birthday figure.
- Four historic events that took place during the featured month.

Use a two-pyramid diorama to:
- Compare and contrast two holiday celebrations.

Two-Pyramid Diorama

Four-Pyramid Dioramas

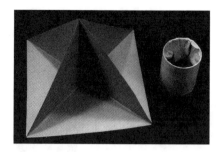

Make a tree trunk by covering a small can (soup cans work well) with brown paper.
Place a green four-pyramid diorama on top.
Decorate the pyramid holiday tree for every season.

Small, medium, and large pyramids can be stacked with the help of ice cream sticks to make a holiday tree.

Two small pyramid dioramas can be glued together to make 3-D, diamond shaped holiday tree ornaments.

41

Holiday Milk Carton Boxes

1. Make a garland as described on page 37 of this book.
2. Glue it around a half pint milk carton to make a small holiday box.

Use the box to hold:
- Party snacks and treats
- Small holiday notes made from the small patterns in this book
- Crayons or art supplies
- Nature collections: rocks, leaves, shells, insects, etc.

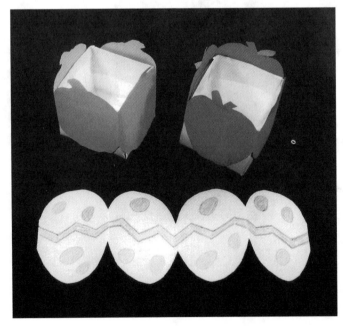

Add a ribbon or pipe cleaner handle to make small holiday baskets. Fill with raffia or shredded tissue paper.

Drinking Cup Pockets

See page 56 of *Dinah Zike's Big Book of Books and Activities*
for fold instructions and academic applications for this book.

Use these drinking cup pockets to hold:
-A bouquet of flowers for Mother's Day. (See page86.)
-Seasonal holiday notes or Valentines.
-A small present wrapped in tissue paper.
-Homemade stationery.
-Holiday vocabulary words.

January

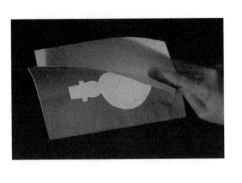

New Year's Day = January 1

Chinese New Year
(Month-long celebration between January 10 and February 19)

Martin Luther King, Jr. Birthday = Third Monday

Inauguration Day = January 20
(Every fourth year)

January Birthdays

Important Note: It is nearly impossible to verify the actual date of birth of many historic figures. Different sources give differing dates for several birthdays in this list. The birth years listed are more accurate than the birth months or days.

January 3, 1793: Lucretia Coffin Mott, American leader of woman's suffrage and equal rights for women.
January 4, 1809: Louis Braille, blind American teacher and inventor was born in France.
January 4, 1785: Jacob Grimm, German compiler of fairy tales.
January 6, 1412: Joan of Arc, French martyr and saint.
January 6, 1878: Carl Sandburg, American poet and biographer.
January 6, 1957: Nancy Lopez-Melton, American golf champion.
January 7, 1800: Millard Fillmore, 13th U. S. President.
January 8, 1935: Elvis Presley, popular American singer.
January 9, 1913: Richard Milhouse Nixon, 37th U. S. President.
January 12, 1920: James Farmer, American civil rights leader.
January 12, 1628: Charles Perrault, French author of *Cinderella* and *Sleeping Beauty*.
January 12, 1876: Jack London, American author of *Call of the Wild*.
January 12, 1856: John Singer Sargent, American painter.
January 13, 1912: Woody Guthrie, American folk singer.
January 14, 1875: Albert Schweitzer, German-born physician, humanitarian, and African missionary.
January 14, 1741: Benedict Arnold, American Revolutionary war traitor.
January 14, 1940: Julian Bond, Black American civil rights activist and politician.
January 15, 1929: Dr. Martin Luther King, American clergyman, civil rights leader, and Nobel Prize winner.
January 15, 1622: Moliere, (Jean Baptist Poquelin) French dramatist and author of comedies.
January 17, 1706: Benjamin Franklin, American inventor, printer, scientist, writer, and statesman.
January 17, 1931: James Earl Jones, American actor.
January 18, 1882: A.A. Milne, creator of *Winnie the Pooh*.
January 19, 1807: Robert E. Lee, U. S. Confederate general.
January 19, 1839: Paul Cezanne, French Impressionist painter.
January 19, 1809: Edgar Allen Poe, American mystery writer, poet, and literary critic.
January 21, 1824: Thomas Jonathan "Stonewall" Jackson, U. S. Confederate general.
January 22, 1788: Lord George Byron, English romantic poet.
January 23, 1832: Edouard Manet, French Impressionist painter.
January 23, 1737: John Hancock, first signer of the U. S. Declaration of Independence.
January 24, 1925: Maria Tallchief, Native American ballerina.
January 25, 1759: Robert Burns, Scottish poet and songwriter (*Auld Lang Syne*).
January 25, 1882: Virginia Woolf, English author and critic.
January 27, 1756: Wolfgang Mozart, German composer.
January 27, 1832: Louis Carroll, English mathematician and author of *Alice in Wonderland*.
January 27, 1948: Mikhail Baryshnikov, Russian ballet dancer.
January 28, 1912: Jackson Pollack, American abstract painter.
January 29, 1843: William McKinley, 25th U. S. President.
January 30, 1882: Franklin Delano Roosevelt, 32nd U. S. President.
January 31, 1885: Anna Pavlova, Russian ballerina.
January 31, 1919: Jackie Robinson, first Black American major league baseball player.

Use full-page patterns for:
-Desk Top Projects
-Cereal Box Covers
-Large Accordion Books
-Display Cubes
-Giant Ornaments

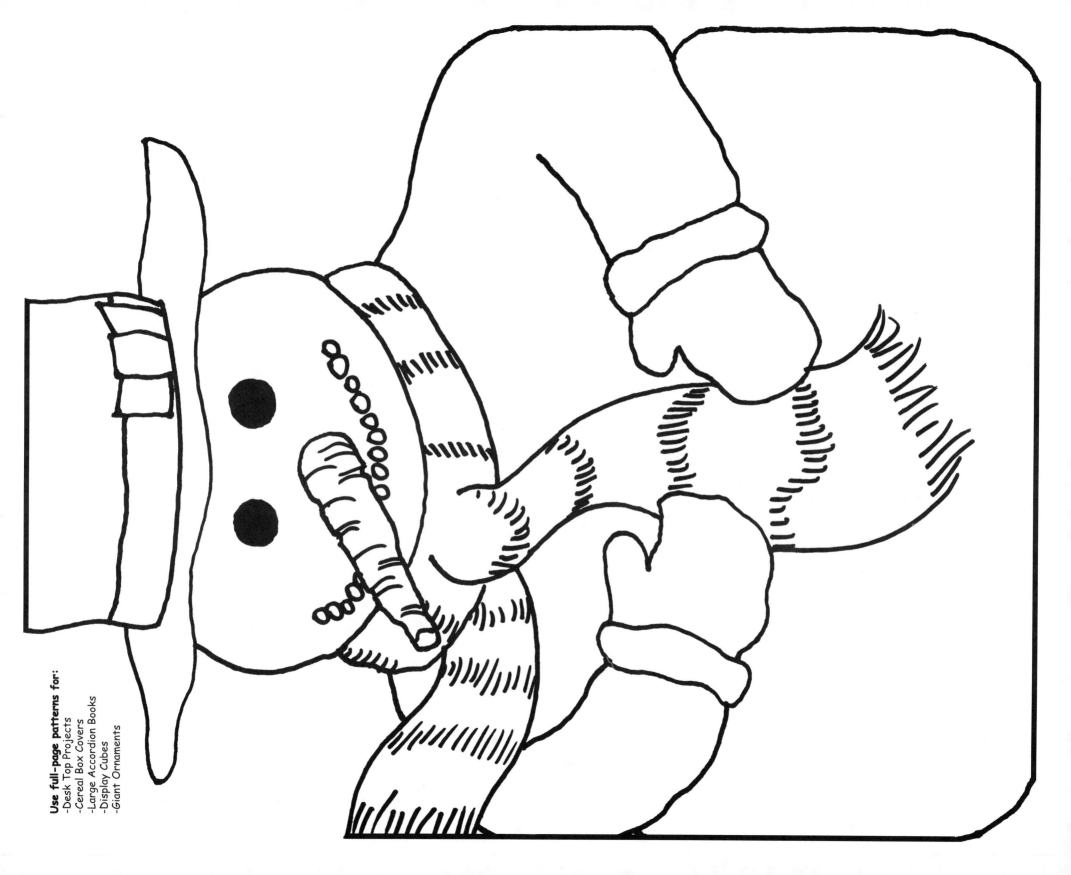

Use full-page patterns for:
-Desk Top Projects
-Cereal Box Covers
-Large Accordion Books
-Display Cubes
-Giant Ornaments

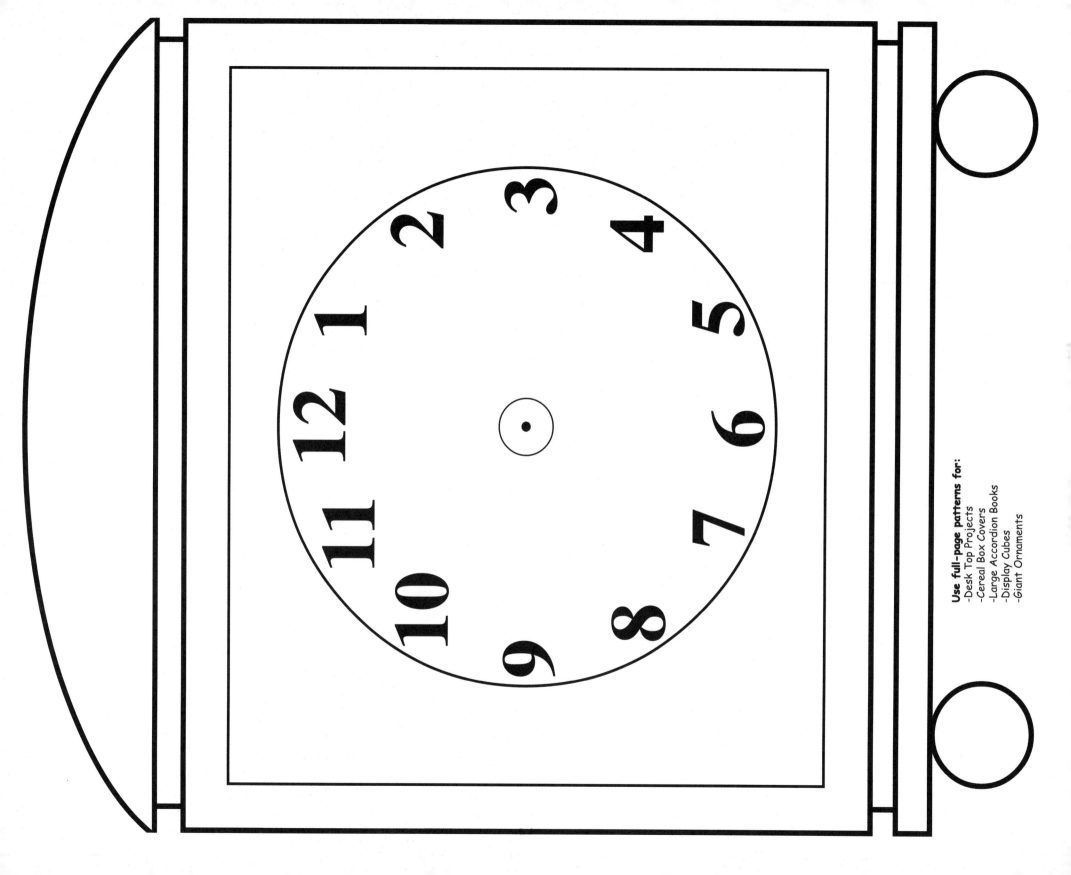

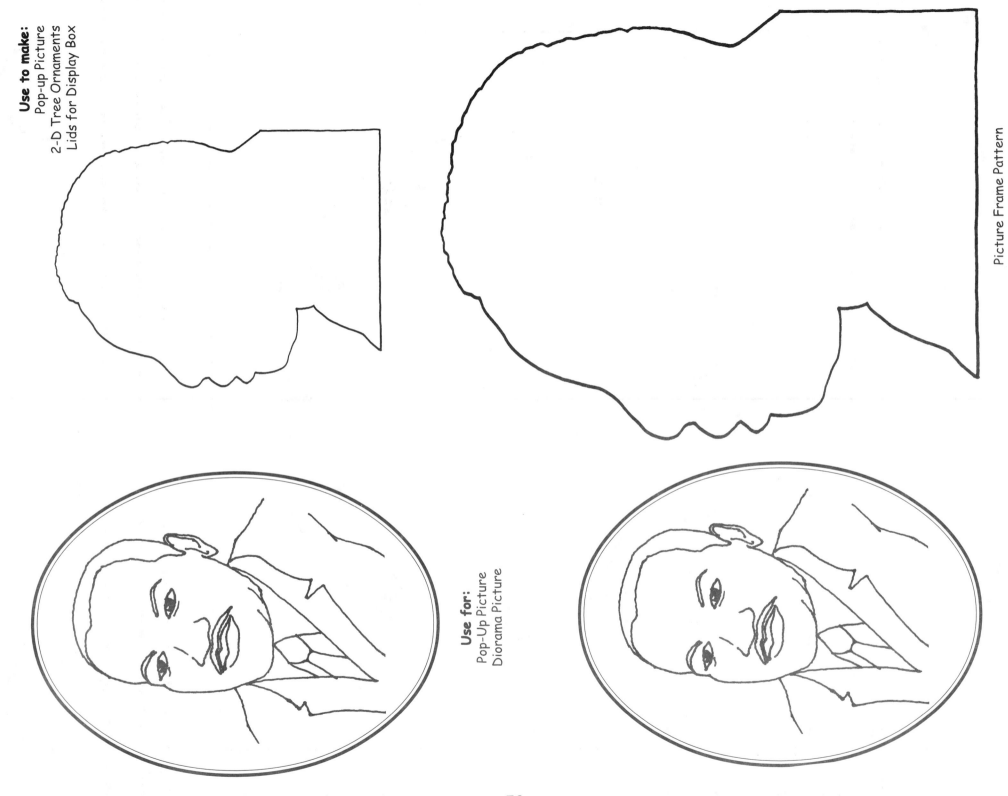

Picture Frame Pattern

Use for:
Pop-Up Picture
Diorama Picture

50

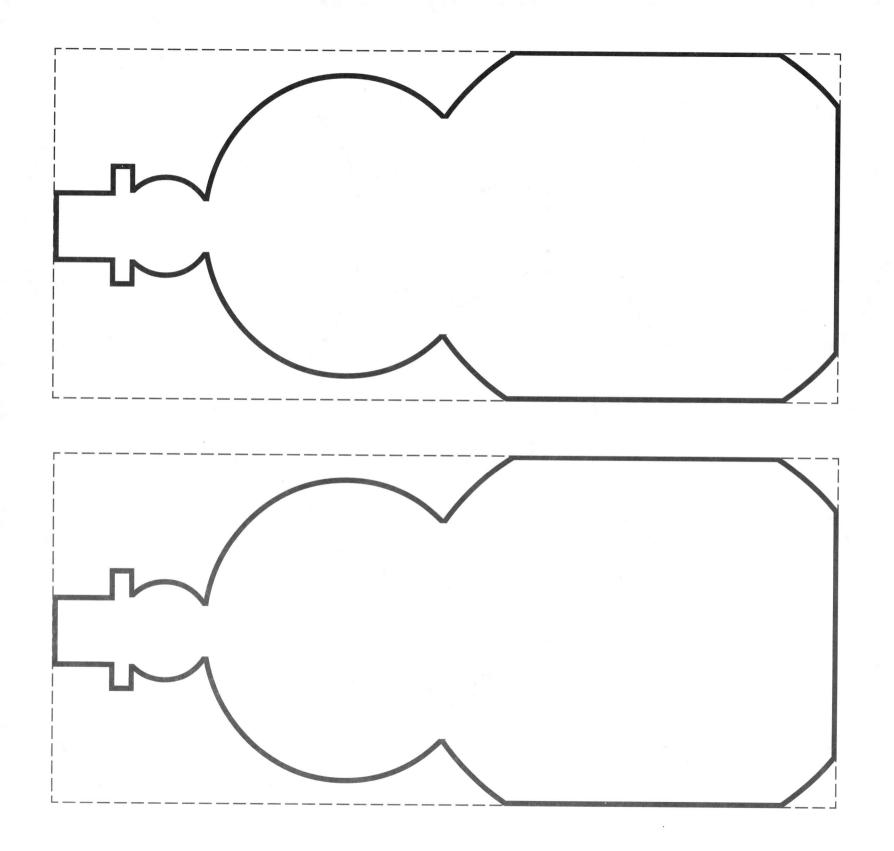

Use to make:
Trifold Writing Books
Trifold Garlands

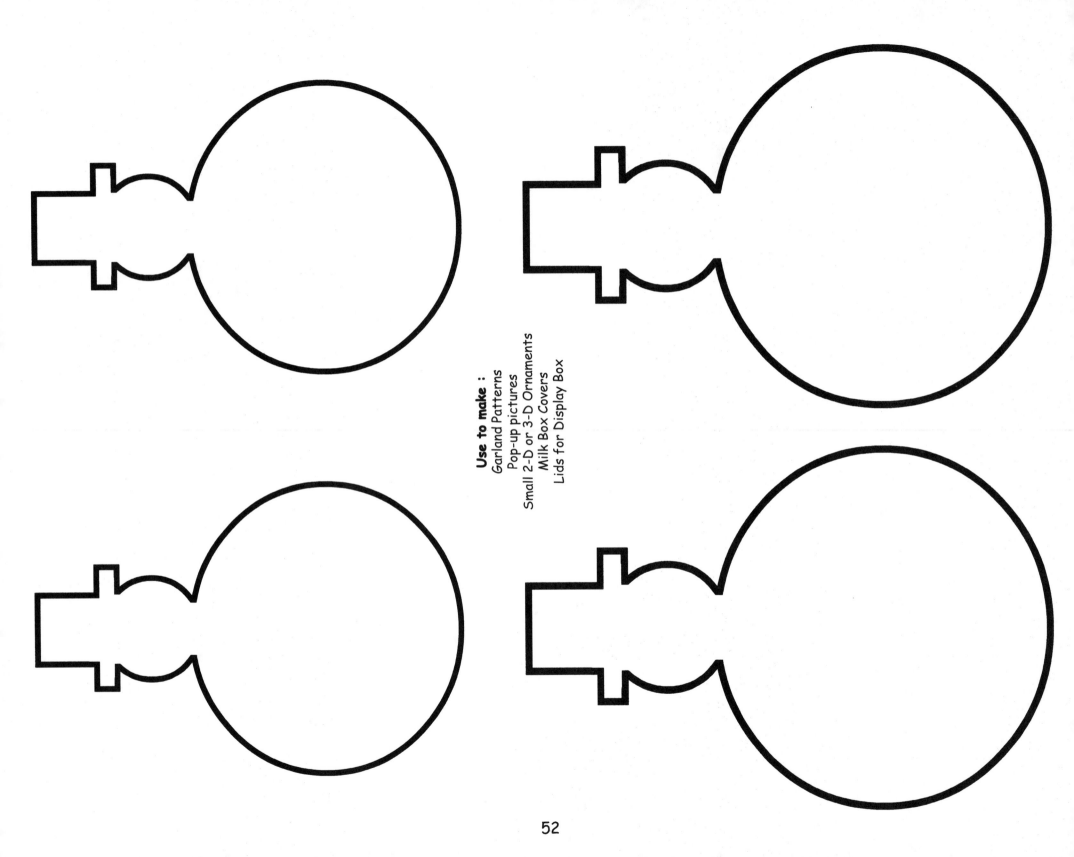

Use to make :
Garland Patterns
Pop-up pictures
Small 2-D or 3-D Ornaments
Milk Box Covers
Lids for Display Box

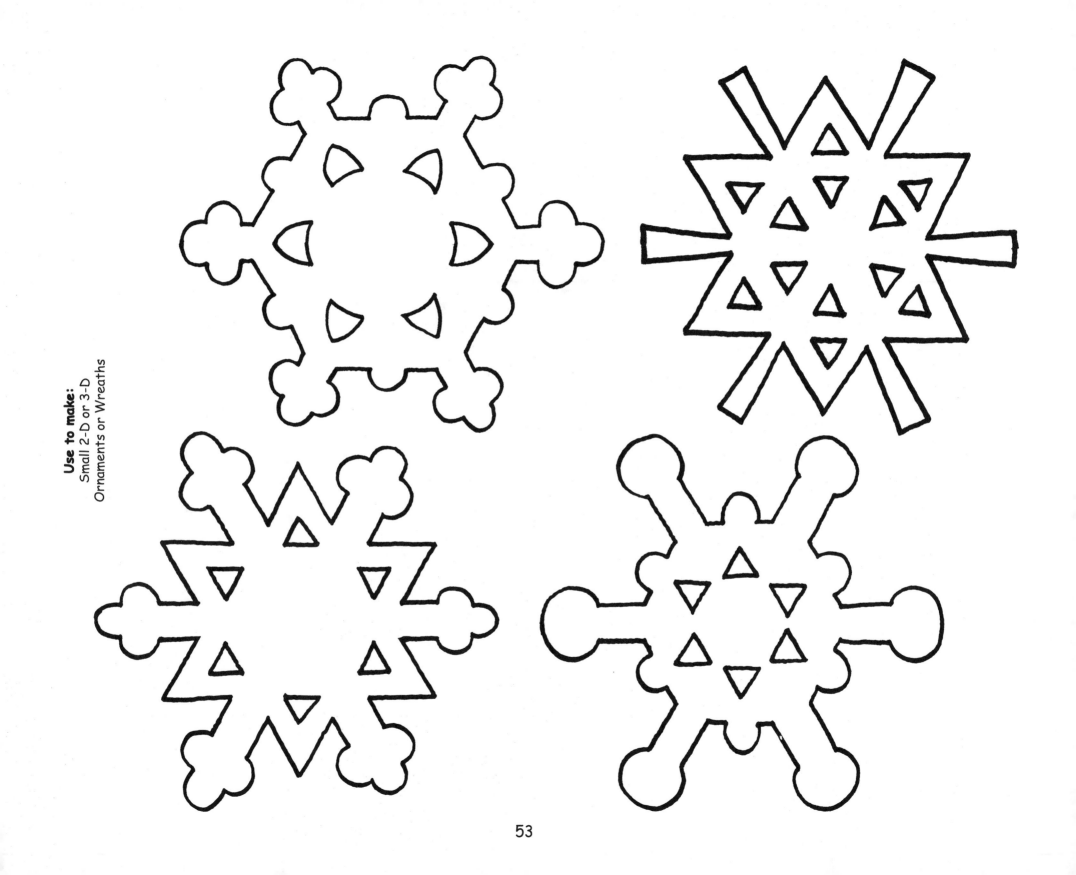

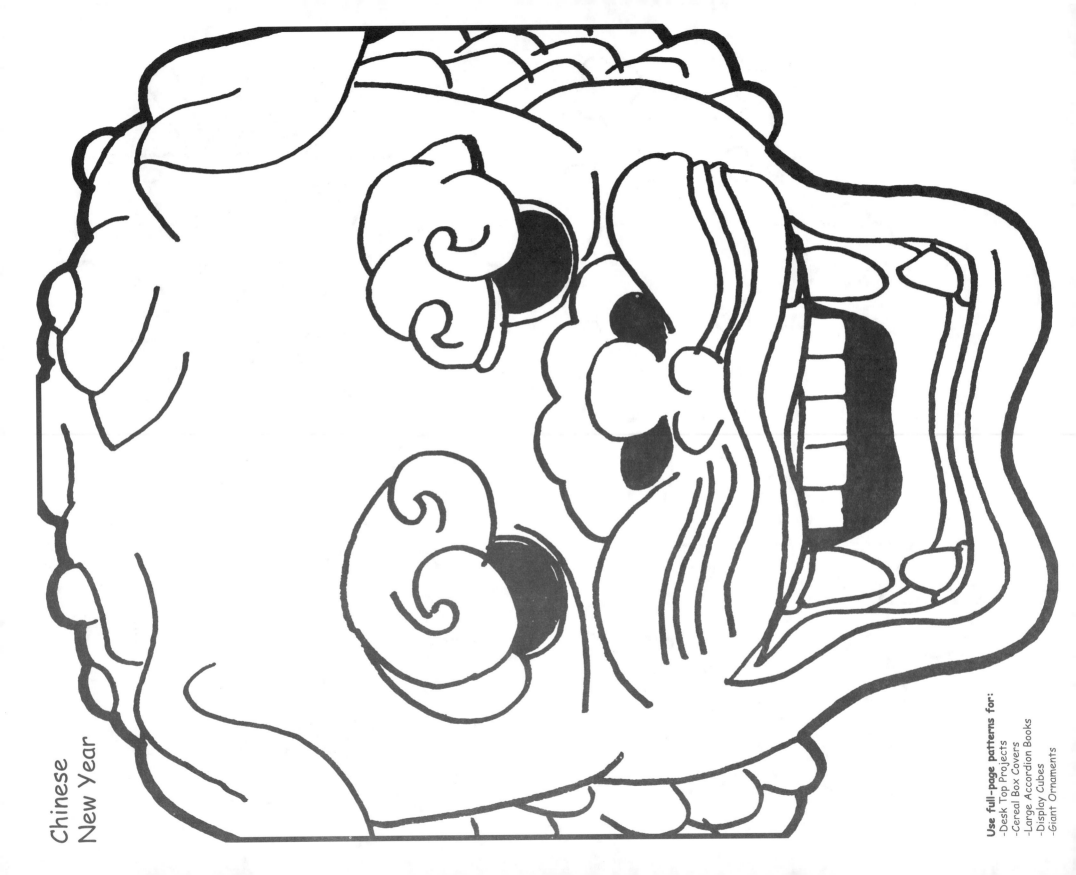

Chinese
New Year

February

Black History Month

National Children's Dental Health Week = begins first Sunday

National Wildlife Week = begins third Sunday

Leap Year
(Occurs in years when the last two digits are evenly divisible by 4)

Groundhog Day = February 2

Valentine's Day = February 14

President's Day = Third Monday
(Celebrates President Lincoln and Washington's birthdays)

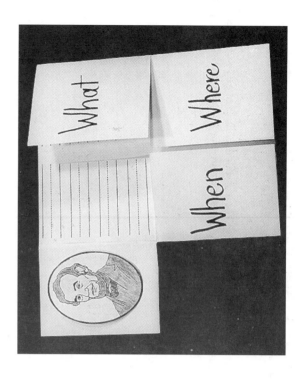

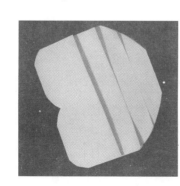

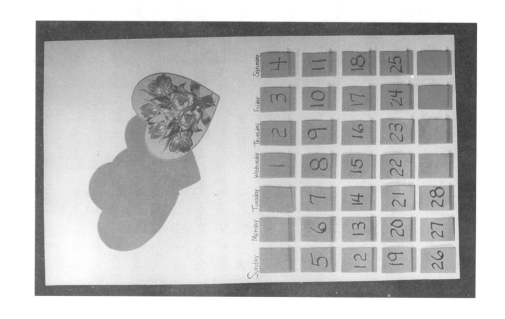

February Birthdays

Use For: Creative Writing Papers; Research Projects: Timelines/Timetables, & Geography Integration

Important Note: It is nearly impossible to verify the actual date of birth of many historic figures. Different sources give differing dates for several birthdays in this list. The birth years listed are more accurate than the birth months or days.

February 2, 1882: James Joyce, Irish author.
February 3, 1809: Felix Mendelssohn, German composer.
February 4, 1902: Charles Lindberg, American aviator.
February 4, 1934: Hank Aaron, Black American baseball player.
February 6, 1895: George "Babe" Ruth, American baseball player
February 6, 1911: Ronald Reagan, 40th U. S. President.
February 7, 1812: Charles Dickens, English novelist.
February 7, 1885: Sinclair Lewis, American novelist.
February 7, 1867: Laura Ingalls Wilder, American author.
February 8, 1828: Jules Verne, French science-fiction writer.
February 9, 1773: William H. Harrison, 9th U. S. President.
February 11, 1847: Thomas A. Edison, American inventor.
February 12, 1809: Abraham Lincoln, 16th U. S. President.
February 12, 1809, Charles Darwin, English naturalist.
February 13, 1892: Grant Wood, American painter.
February 14, 1817: Frederick Douglas, Black American leader.
February 15, 1564: Galileo Galilei, Italian scientist.
February 15, 1820: Susan B. Anthony, American feminist.
February 19, 1473: Nicolaus Copernicus, Polish astronomer.
February 21, 1936: Barbara Jordan, black politician and teacher.
February 22, 1732: George Washington, 1st U. S. President.
February 22, 1810: Frederic Chopin, Polish composer.
February 22, 1819: James Russell Lowell, American poet and lawyer.
February 22, 1892: Edna St. Vincent Millay, American lyrical poet.
February 23, 1787: Emma Willard, American educator and pioneer in women's education.
February 24, 1658: George Frederick Handel, British composer.
February 24, 1836: Winslow Homer, American marine artist.
February 24, 1786: Wilhelm Grimm, German writer of children's stories.
February 25, 1841: Pierre Auguste Renoir, French impressionist painter.
February 25, 1822: Hiram Rhoades Revels, clergyman and first Black American Senator.
February 26, 1846: William Cody (Bullafo Bill), American scout and showman.
February 26, 1902: John Steinbeck, American writer.
February 26, 1802: Victor Hugo, French poet, novelist, and dramatist.
February 27, 1807: Henry Wadsworth Longfellow, American poet.
February 27, 1934: N. Scott Momaday, American Indian writer.
February 28, 1901: Linus Pauling, American chemist and Nobel Peace Prize winner.

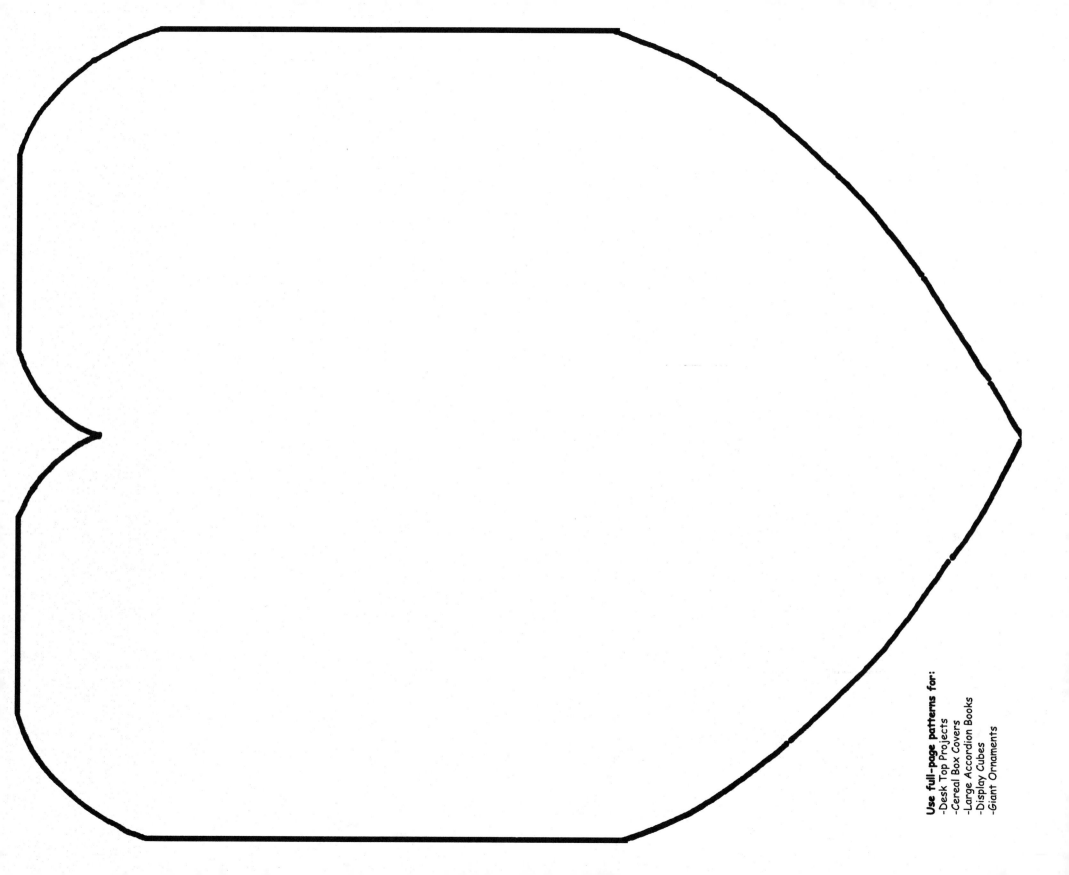

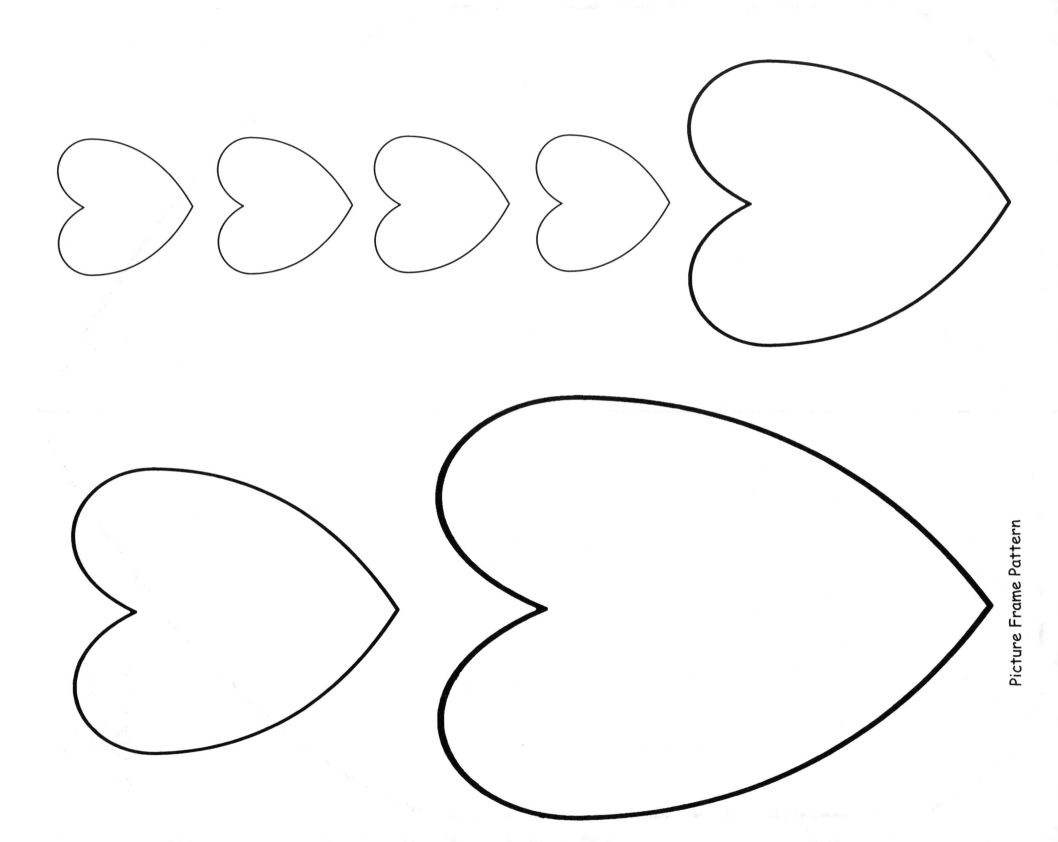

Picture Frame Pattern

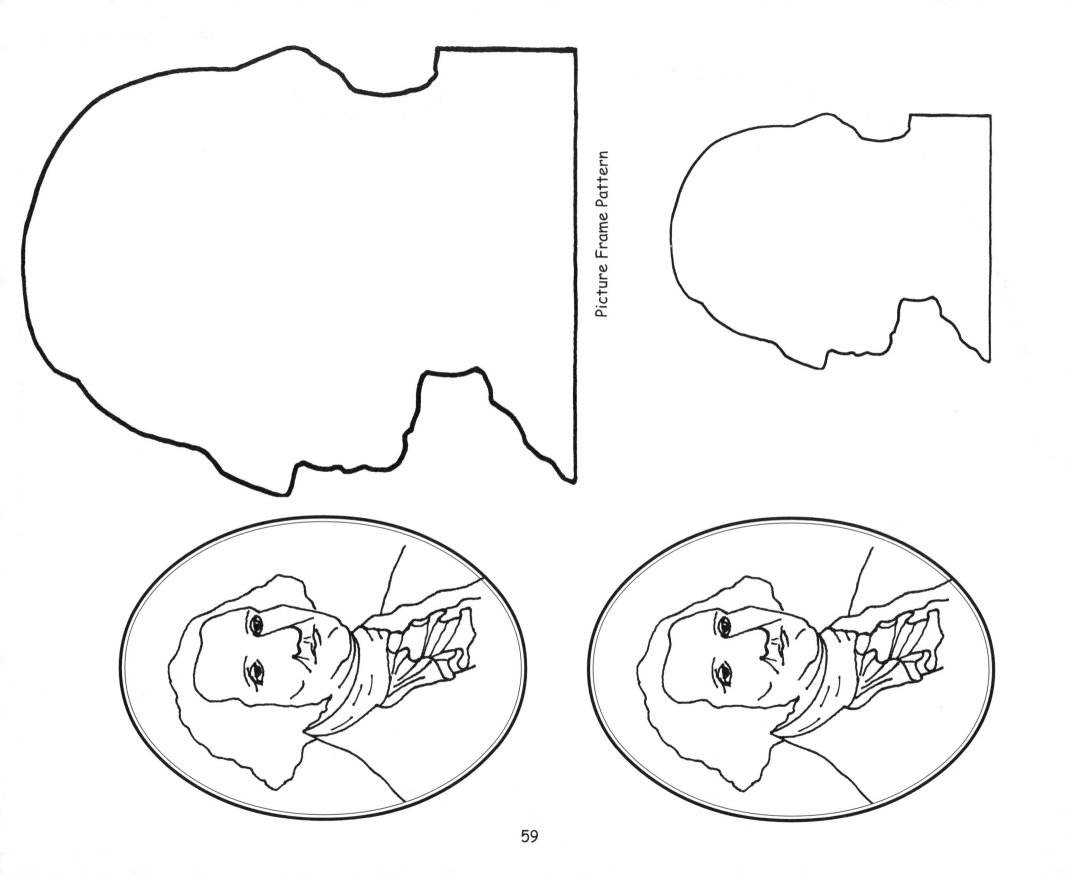

Picture Frame Pattern

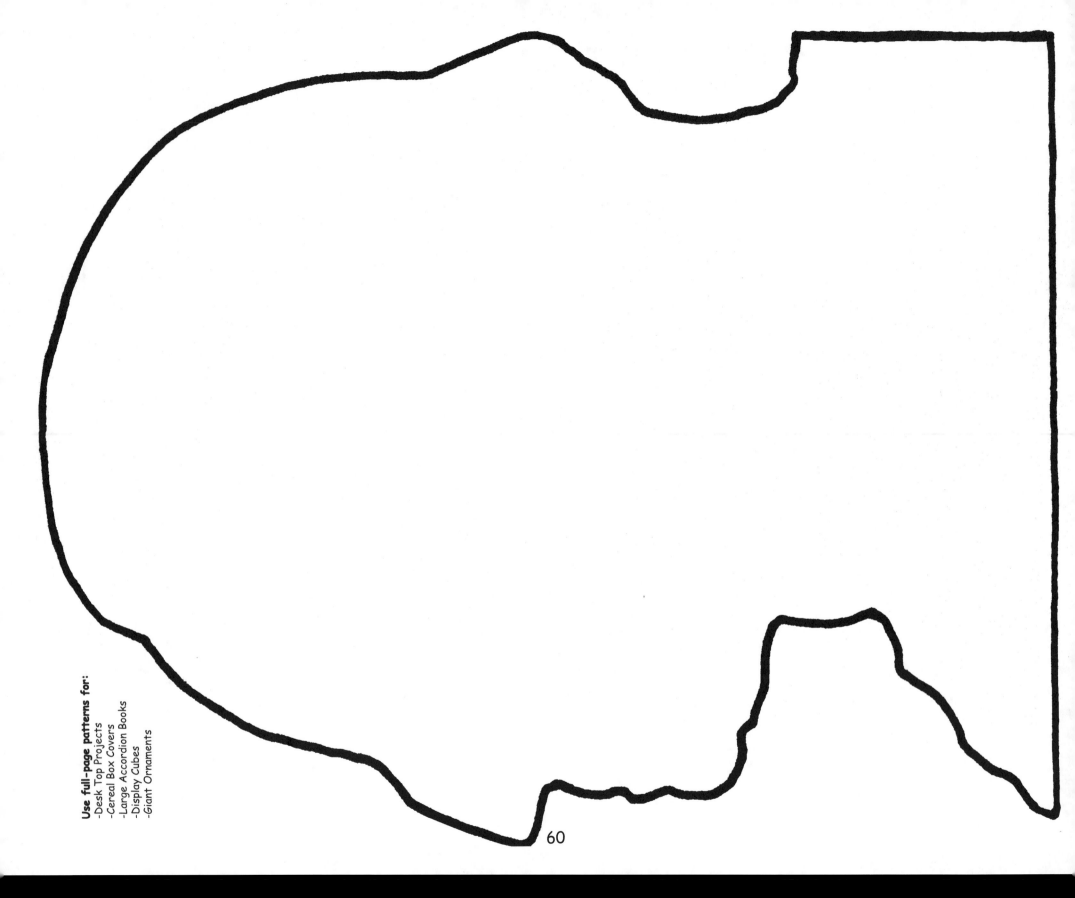

Use full-page patterns for:
-Desk Top Projects
-Cereal Box Covers
-Large Accordion Books
-Display Cubes
-Giant Ornaments

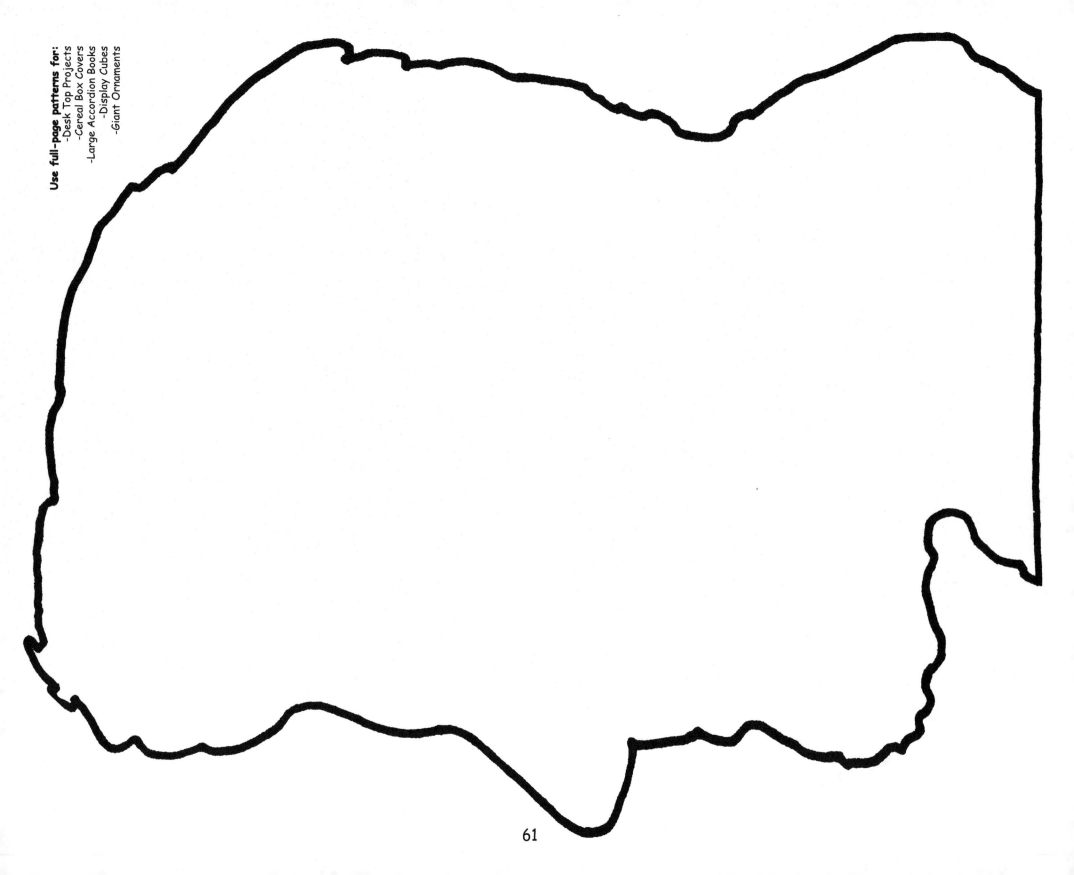

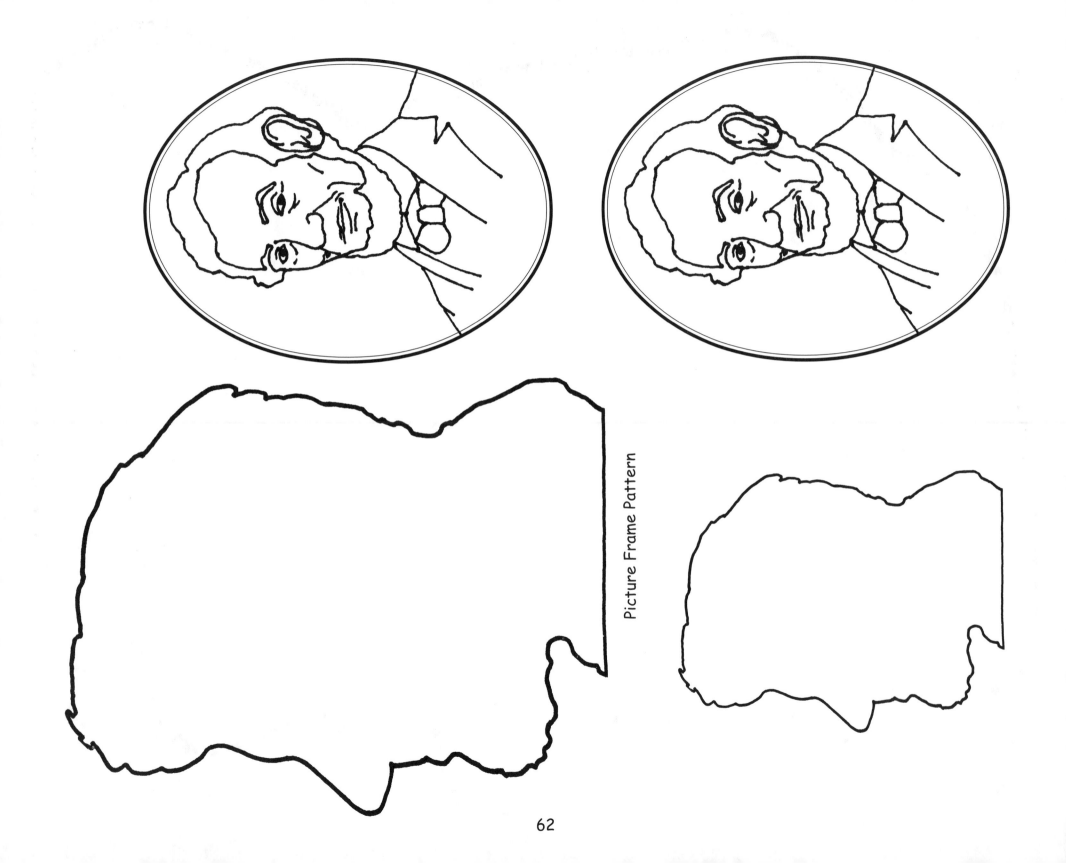

Picture Frame Pattern

62

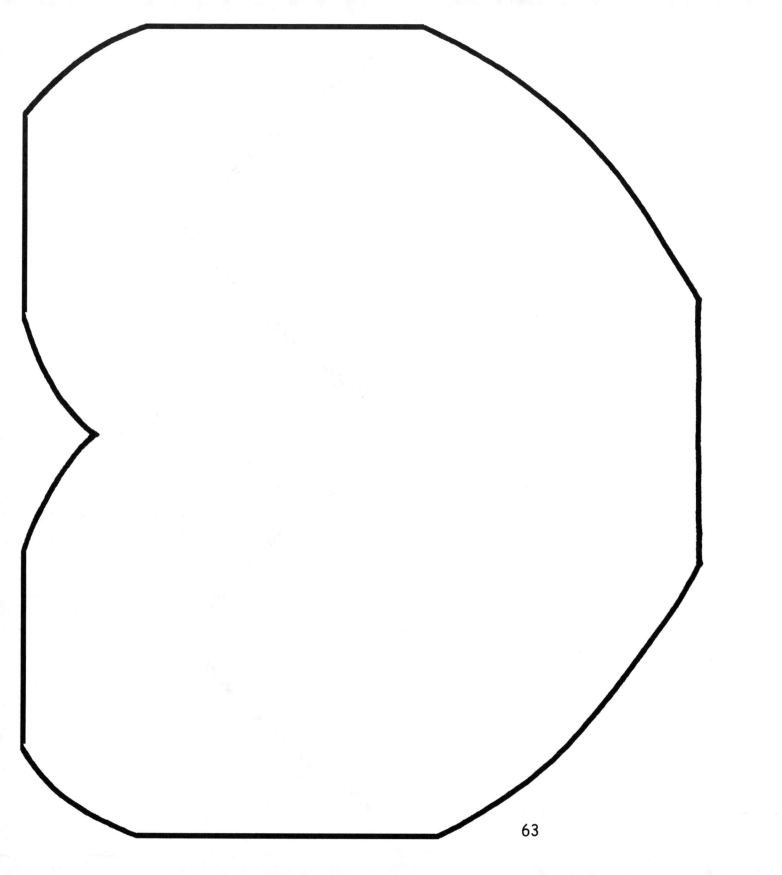

Use to make patterns for
layered-look books

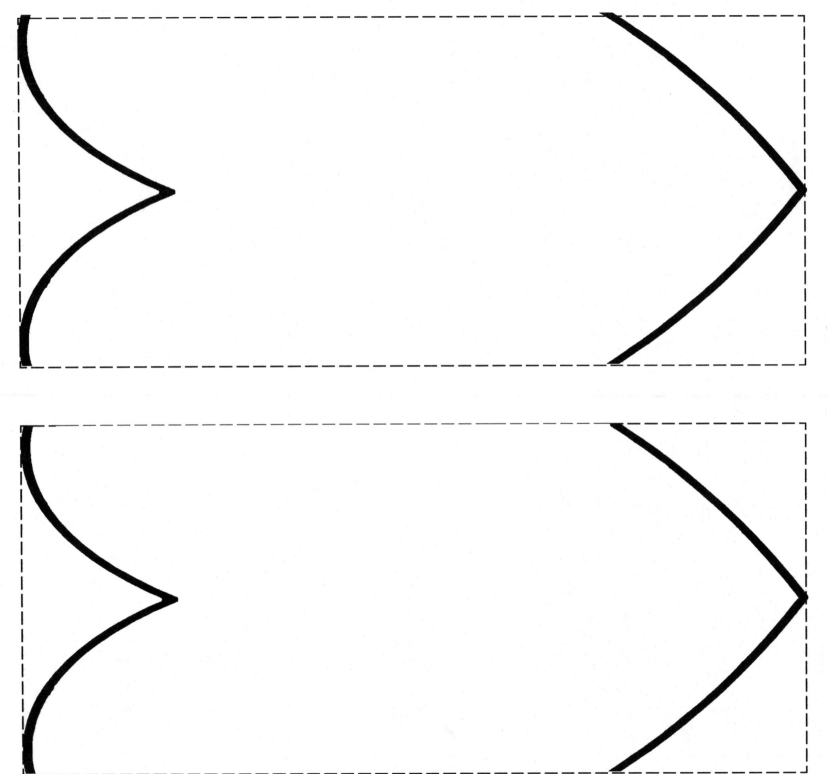

March

Youth Art Month

Red Cross Month

Passover and Easter
(March or April)

Dolls Day (Japan) = March 3

International Women's Day = March 8

The Ides of March = March 15
(Julius Caesar assassinated, 44 B.C.)

St. Patrick's Day = March 17

Daylight Savings Time = last Sunday of the Month
(Where applicable)

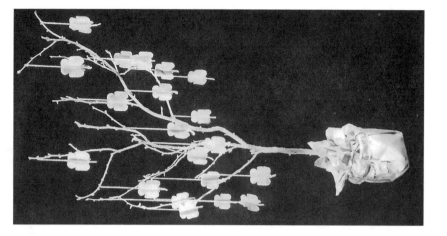

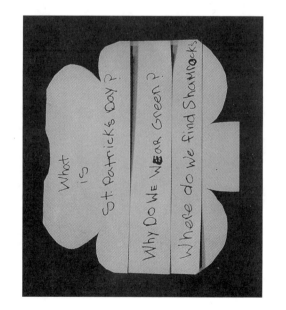

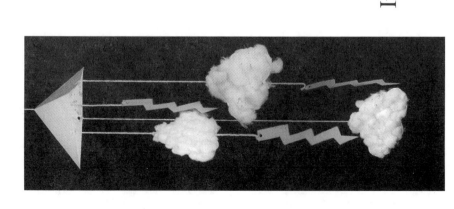

March Birthdays

Use For: Creative Writing Papers; Research Projects: Timelines/Timetables, & Geography Integration

Important Note: It is nearly impossible to verify the actual date of birth of many historic figures. Different sources give differing dates for several birthdays in this list. The birth years listed are more accurate than the birth months or days.

March 1, 1914: Ralph Ellison, Black American author.
March 3, 1847: Alexander Graham Bell, Scottish-American teacher, scientist, and inventor
March 4, 1678: Antonio Vivaldi, Italian composer.
March 4, 1904: Theodor Geisel (Dr. Seuss), American author, artist, publisher.
March 5, 1512: Gerard Mercator, geographer.
March 6, 1475: Michelangelo, Italian painter and sculptor.
March 6, 1806: Elizabeth Barrett Browning, English poet.
March 6, 1619: Cyrano de Bergerac, French playwright and soldier.
March 7, 1875: Maurice Ravel, French composer.
March 7, 1849: Luther Burbank, American botanist and horticulturist.
March 8, 1841: Oliver Wendell Holmes, Jr., Associate Justice of Supreme Court.
March 9, 1454: Amerigo Vespucci, Italian explorer.
March 10, 1820: Harriet Tubman, Black American abolitionist.
March 11, 1847: Johnny Appleseed (Jonathan Chapman), died.
March 14, 1825: Johann Strauss, Austrian composer.
March 14, 1879: Albert Einstein, German-born, American scientist.
March 15, 1767: Andrew Jackson, 7th U. S. President.
March 16, 1751: James Madison, 4th U. S. President.
March 16, 1787: George Ohm, German physicist.
March 18, 1837: Grover Cleveland, 22nd & 24th U. S. President.
March 18, 1858: Rudolph Diesel, German engineer.
March 19, 1860: William Jennings Bryan, American lawyer and political leader.
March 21, 1685: Johann Sebastian Bach, German composer.
March 22, 1599: Anthony Van Dyck, Flemish painter.
March 22, 1852: Francis Bourdillion, English poet (*The Night Has a Thousand Eyes*).
March 23, 1857: Fannie Farmer, American author of recipes with standardized measurements.
March 24, 1874: Harry Houdini, American magician and escape artist.
March 24, 1820: Frances Crosby, blind poet and author of thousands of hymns.
March 25, 1871: Gutzon Borglum, American sculptor of Mount Rushmore.
March 26, 1874: Robert Frost, American poet.
March 27, 1813: Nathaniel Currier, American lithographer.
March 27, 1879: Edward Steichen, American photographer.
March 29, 1790: John Tyler, 10th U. S. President.
March 30, 1746: Francisco Goya, Spanish painter.
March 30, 1853: Vincent van Gogh, Dutch painter.
March 30, 1820: Anna Wewell, author of *Black Beauty*.
March 31, 1732: Joseph Haydn, Austrian composer.
March 31, 1927: Caesar Chavez, Hispanic labor leader.

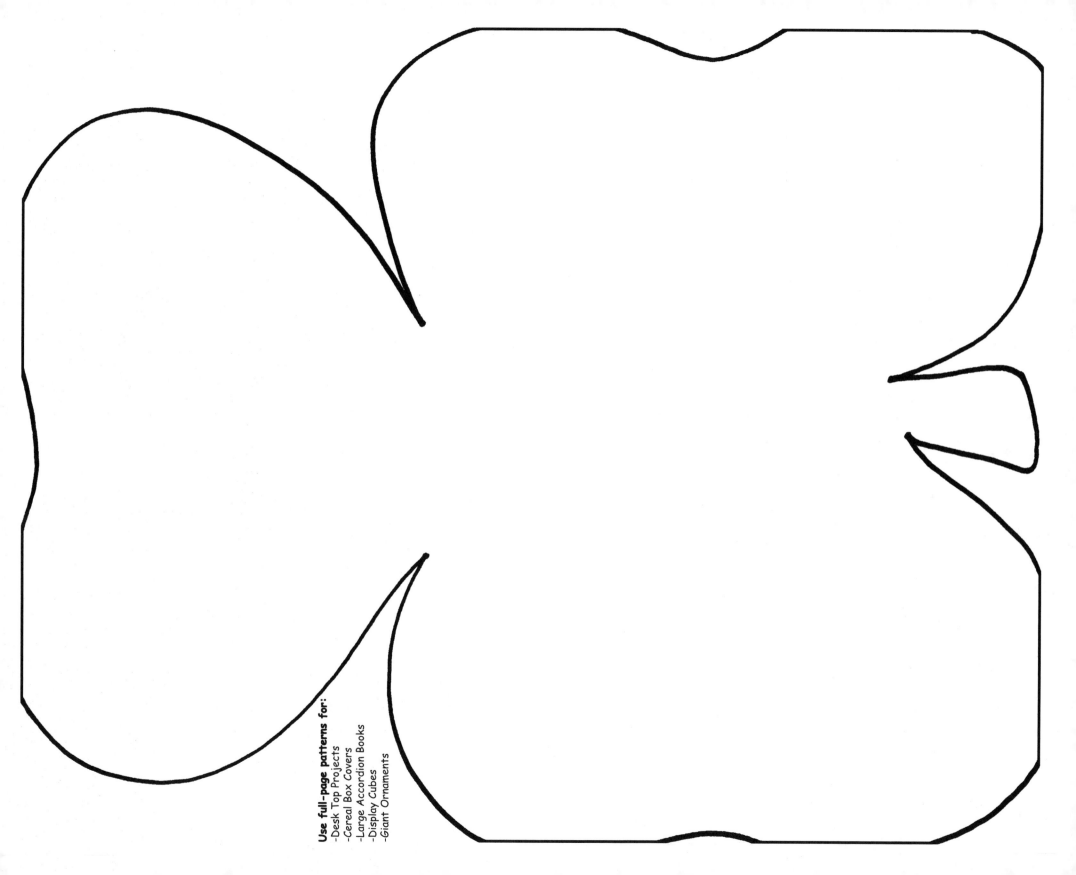

Use full-page patterns for:
-Desk Top Projects
-Cereal Box Covers
-Large Accordion Books
-Display Cubes
-Giant Ornaments

Use small shamrocks for:
- Garland Patterns
- Pop-up pictures
- Small 2-D or 3-D Ornaments
- Milk Box Covers
- Cutout lids for Display Box

Use medium-sized shamrocks for:
- Picture Frame Books
- Large 2-D or 3-D ornaments

Use to make patterns for:
Layered-look Books

Use to make 2-D ornaments for:
-'spring shower' mobiles
-weather mobiles

April

Palm Sunday and Good Friday (March or April)

Easter

(March or April: Celebrated on the 1st Sunday following the full moon that falls on or after March 21st)

April Fool's Day = April 1

International Children's Book Day = April 2

Flower Festival (Japan) = April 8

National Library Week = begins third Sunday

National Arbor Day = April 22
(Can vary from state to state)

Earth Day = April 22

Public Schools Week (dates vary)

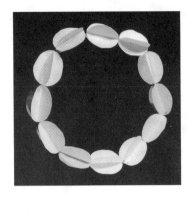

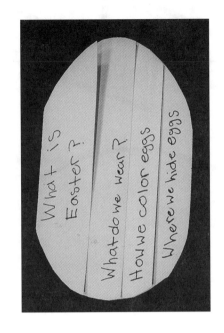

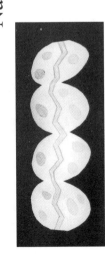

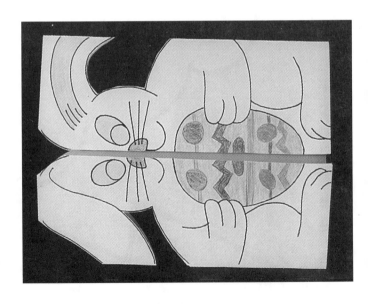

April Birthdays

Use For: Creative Writing Papers; Research Projects;
Timelines/Timetables, & Geography Integration

Important Note: It is nearly impossible to verify the actual date of birth of many historic figures. Different sources give differing dates for several birthdays in this list. The birth years listed are more accurate than the birth months or days.

April 2, 1805: Hans Christian Andersen, Danish author and collector of fairy tales.
April 2, 1873: Sergei Rachmaninoff, Russian composer.
April 2, 742(?): Charlemagne, creator of the Holy Roman Empire.
April 3, 1934: Jane Goodall, British anthropologist and chimpanzee expert.
April 3, 1783: Washington Irving, American author.
April 3, 1837: John Burroughs, American naturalist.
April 5, 1856: Booker T. Washington, American educator.
April 5, 1921: Alex Haley, Black American writer.
April 5, 1856: Booker T. Washington, Black American educator.
April 7, 1770: William Wordsworth, English poet and philosopher.
April 8, 1460: Juan Ponce de Leon, Spanish explorer.
April 12, 1777: Henry Clay, noted American statesman.
April 12, 1883: Imogen Cunningham, photographer.
April 13, 1743: Thomas Jefferson, 3rd U. S. President.
April 15, 1452: Leonardo da Vinci, Italian painter, sculptor, experimental scientist, and inventor.
April 15, 1843: Henry James, American writer.
April 16, 1867: Wilbur Wright, American inventor.
April 17, 1885: Isak Dinesen, Danish writer (*Out of Africa*).
April 20, 570: Mohammed, founder of Moslem religion.
April 20, 1808: Napoleon III, emperor of France.
April 21, 1838: John Muir, Scottish-born, American naturalist.
April 21, 1926: Queen Elizabeth, II of England.
April 21, 1816: Charlotte Bronte, English author.
April 22, 1822: Edward Everett Hale, American clergyman and author of *The Man Without a Country*.
April 23, 1564(?): William Shakespeare, English playwright and poet.
April 23, 1791: James Buchanan, 15th U. S. President.
April 25, 1599: Oliver Cromwell, leader during the English Civil War and later ruler of England.
April 26, 1785: John James Audobon, American ornithologist and artist.
April 27, 1822: Ulysses S. Grant, Civil War Union general and 18th U. S. President.
April 27, 1791: Samuel Morse, American inventor.
April 28, 1758: James Monroe, 5th U. S. President.

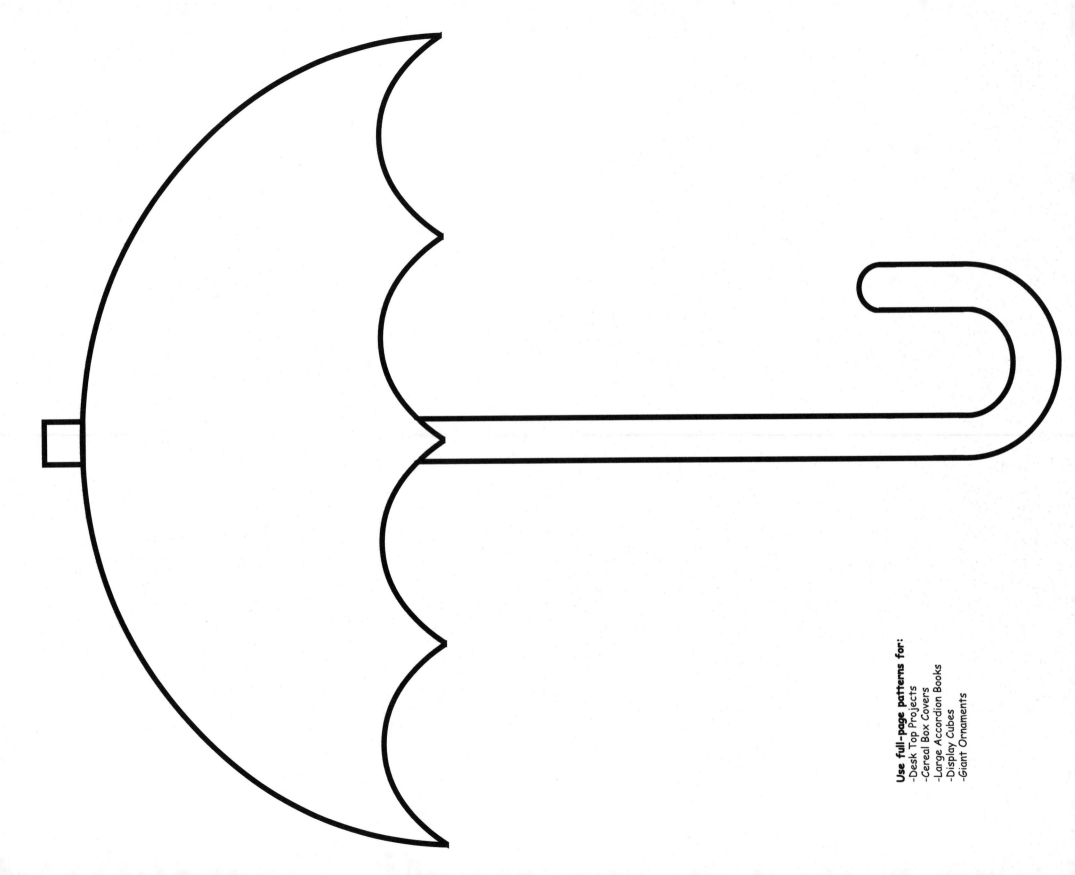

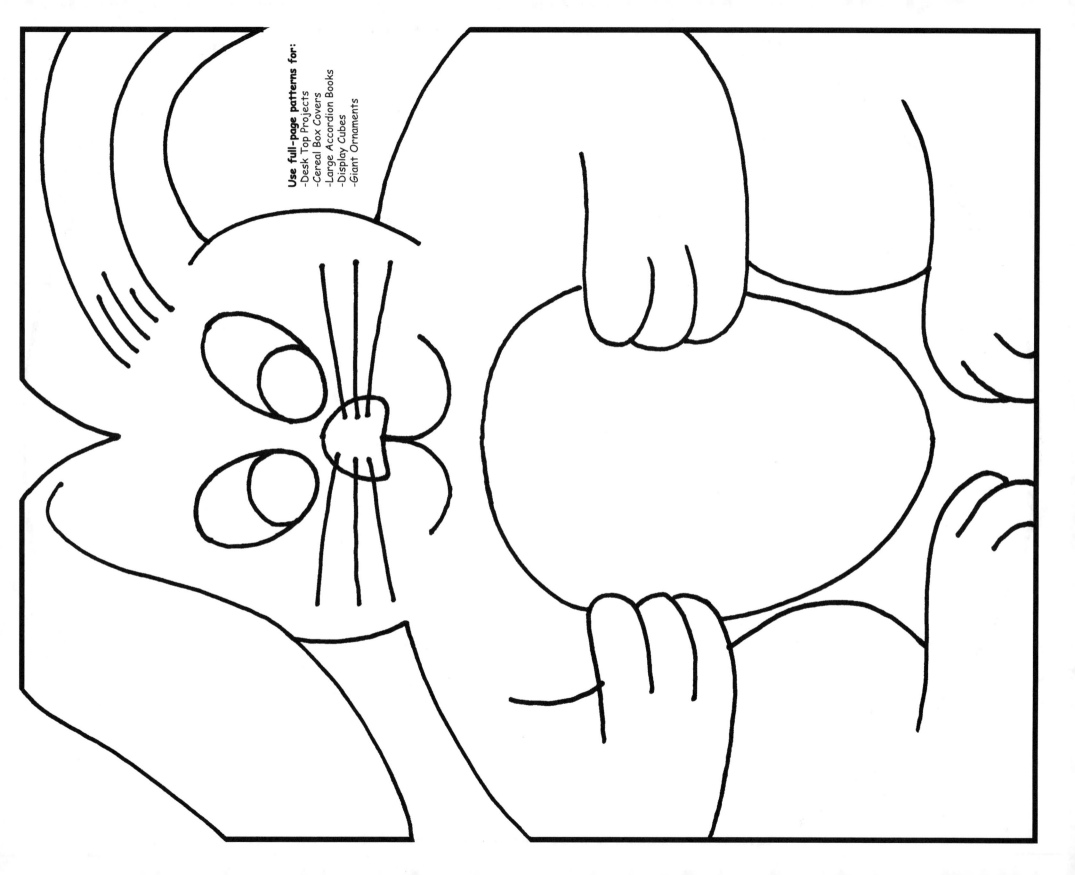

Use full-page patterns for:
-Desk Top Projects
-Cereal Box Covers
-Large Accordion Books
-Display Cubes
-Giant Ornaments

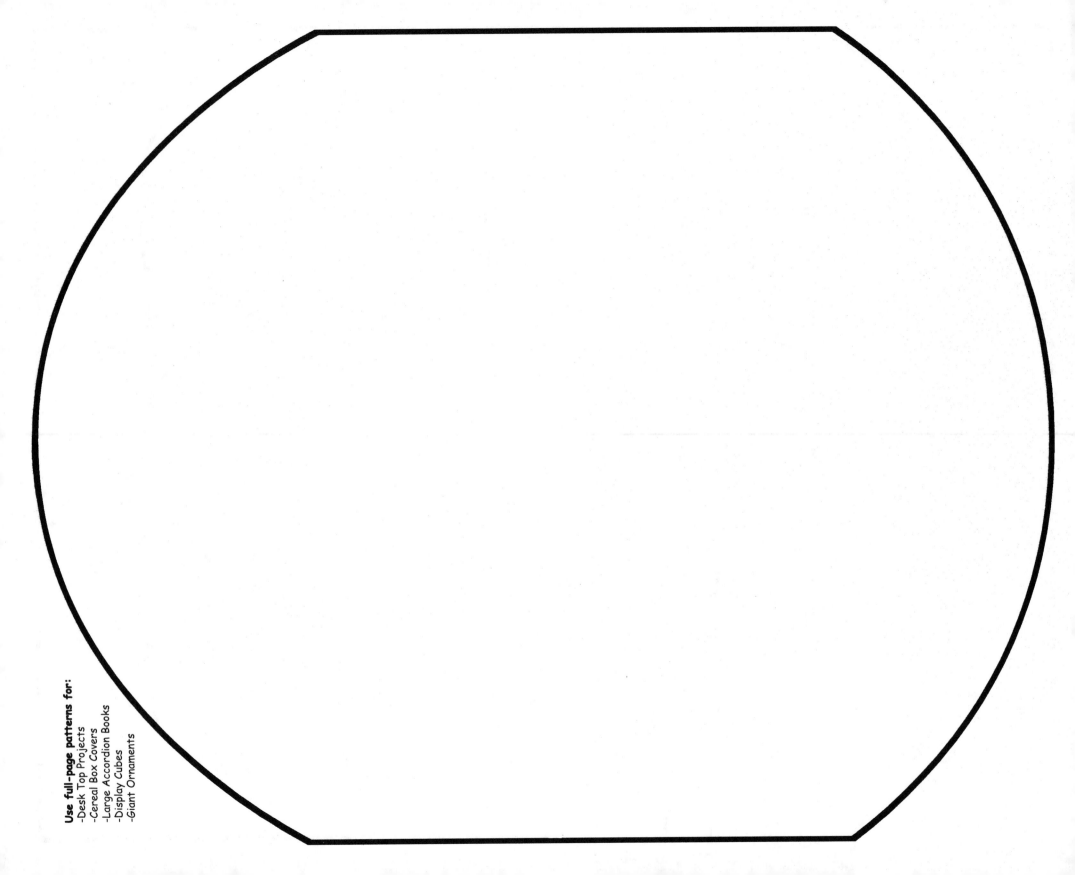

Use full-page patterns for:
-Desk Top Projects
-Cereal Box Covers
-Large Accordion Books
-Display Cubes
-Giant Ornaments

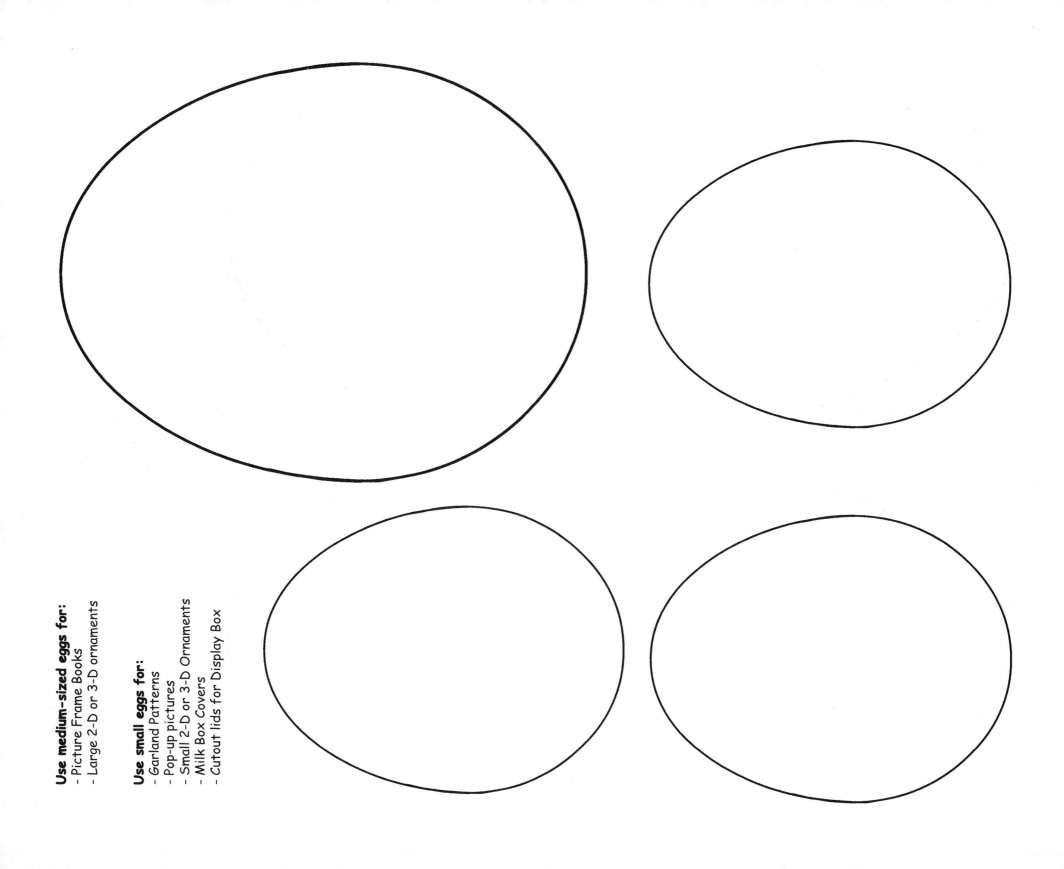

Use medium-sized eggs for:
- Picture Frame Books
- Large 2-D or 3-D ornaments

Use small eggs for:
- Garland Patterns
- Pop-up pictures
- Small 2-D or 3-D Ornaments
- Milk Box Covers
- Cutout lids for Display Box

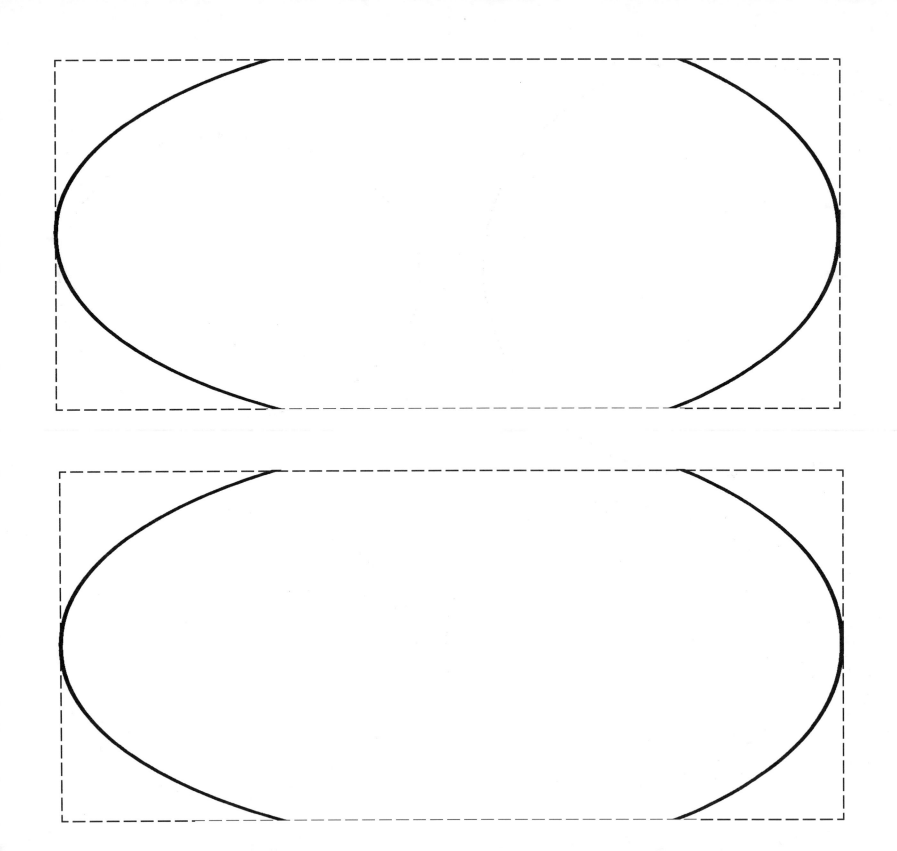

Use to make:
Trifold Books
Trifold Garlands

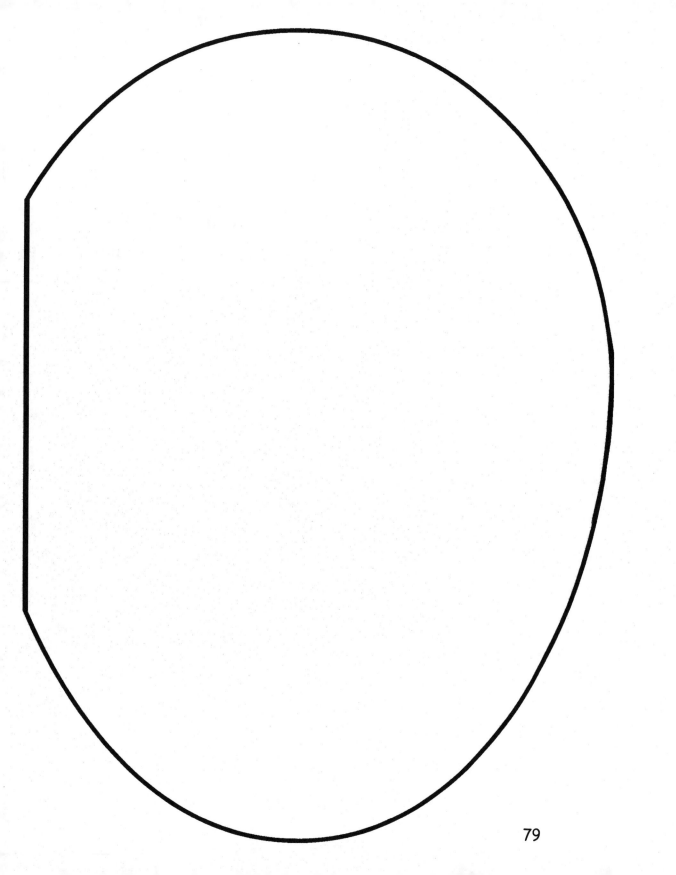

Use to make patterns for:
Layered-look Books

May

Red Cross Month

Senior Citizens Month

May Day = May 1

Cinco de Mayo = May 5
(Commemorates the 1862 defeat of the French by Mexico at the Battle of Pueblo)

Mother's Day = 2nd Sunday in May

World Goodwill Day = May 18

International Museum Day = May 18

National Music Week = begins first Sunday

Be Kind to Animals Week = begins first Sunday

Memorial Day = last Monday in the month

May Birthdays

Use For: *Creative Writing Papers; Research Projects:*
Timelines/Timetables, & Geography Integration

Important Note: It is nearly impossible to verify the actual date of birth of many historic figures. Different sources give differing dates for several birthdays in this list. The birth years listed are more accurate than the birth months or days.

May 2, 1729: Catherine the Great, German-born empress of Russia.
May 3, 1849: Jacob A. Riis, Dutch-American journalist reformer, author of *How the Other Half Lives*.
May 4, 1796: Horace Mann, American educator and reformer.
May 5, 1818: Karl Marx, German philosopher.
May 5, 1867: Nellie Bly, American investigative reporter.
May 6, 1856: Sigmund Freud, Austrian physician and founder of psychoanalysis.
May 6, 1856: Robert E. Peary, Arctic explorer.
May 7, 1812: Robert Browning, English poet husband of Elizabeth Barrett.
May 7, 1833: Johannes Brahms, German composer.
May 7, 1840: Peter Ilich Tchaikovsky, Russian composer.
May 8, 1884: Harry S. Truman, 33rd U. S. President.
May 9, 1860: James M. Barrie, British playwright, novelist, and author of *Peter Pan*.
May 12, 1820: Florence Nightingale, English nurse and founder of modern nursing.
May 12, 1910: Dorothy Crawfoot Hodgkin, Nobel Prize winning British scientist.
May 14, 1686: Gabriel Fahrenheit, German physicist.
May 15, 1859: Pierre Curie, codiscoverer of radium.
May 15, 1930: Jasper Johns, American artist.
May 17, 1749: Dr. Edward Jenner, discoverer of vaccination against smallpox.
May 19, 1864: Carl Akeley, American taxidermist, animal sculptor and naturalist.
May 20, 1768: Dolly Madison, married to U.S. President James Madison.
May 20, 1806: John Stuart Mill, English philosopher, economist, and author of *System of Logic*.
May 21, 1688: Alexander Pope, often quoted English poet. ("To err is human, to forgive divine...")
May 21, 1471: Albrecht Durer, German painter and engraver.
May 22, 1813: Richard Wagner, German composer.
May 22, 1907: Sir Laurence Olivier, English Shakespearean actor and movie star.
May 23, 1707: Carl von Linne (Linnaeus) Swedish naturalist and botanist.
May 23, 1844: Mary Cassatt, American painter of mother & child scenes.
May 24, 1819: Queen Victoria of England.
May 25, 1803: Ralph Waldo Emerson, American poet, essayist, lecturer, and philosopher.
May 26, 1886: Al Jolson, Russian-born American singer and actor who appeared in 'blackface'.
May 27, 1877: Isadora Duncan, American pioneer in modern dance.
May 27, 1907: Rachel Carson, American marine biologist and author of *The Silent Spring*.
May 29, 1736: Patrick Henry, American statesman.
May 29, 1917: John F. Kennedy: 35th U. S. President.
May 31, 1819: Walt Whitman, American poet.

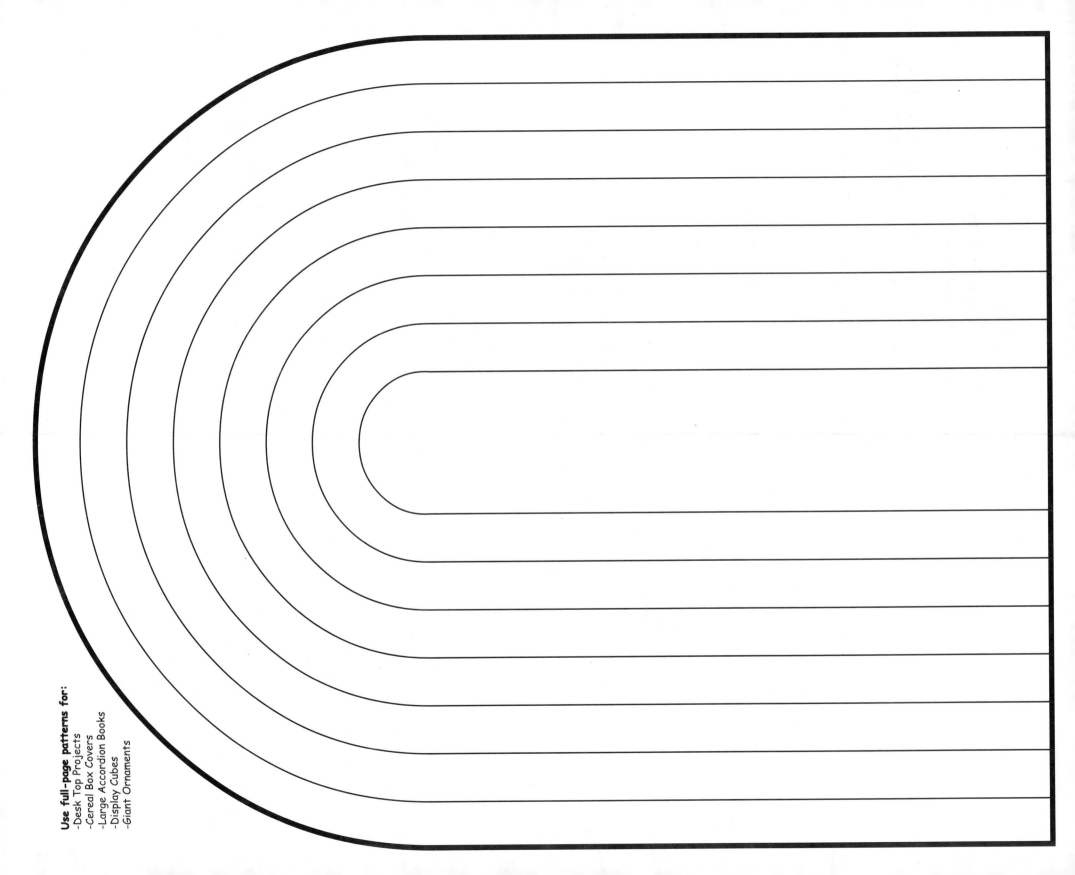

Use full-page patterns for:
-Desk Top Projects
-Cereal Box Covers
-Large Accordion Books
-Display Cubes
-Giant Ornaments

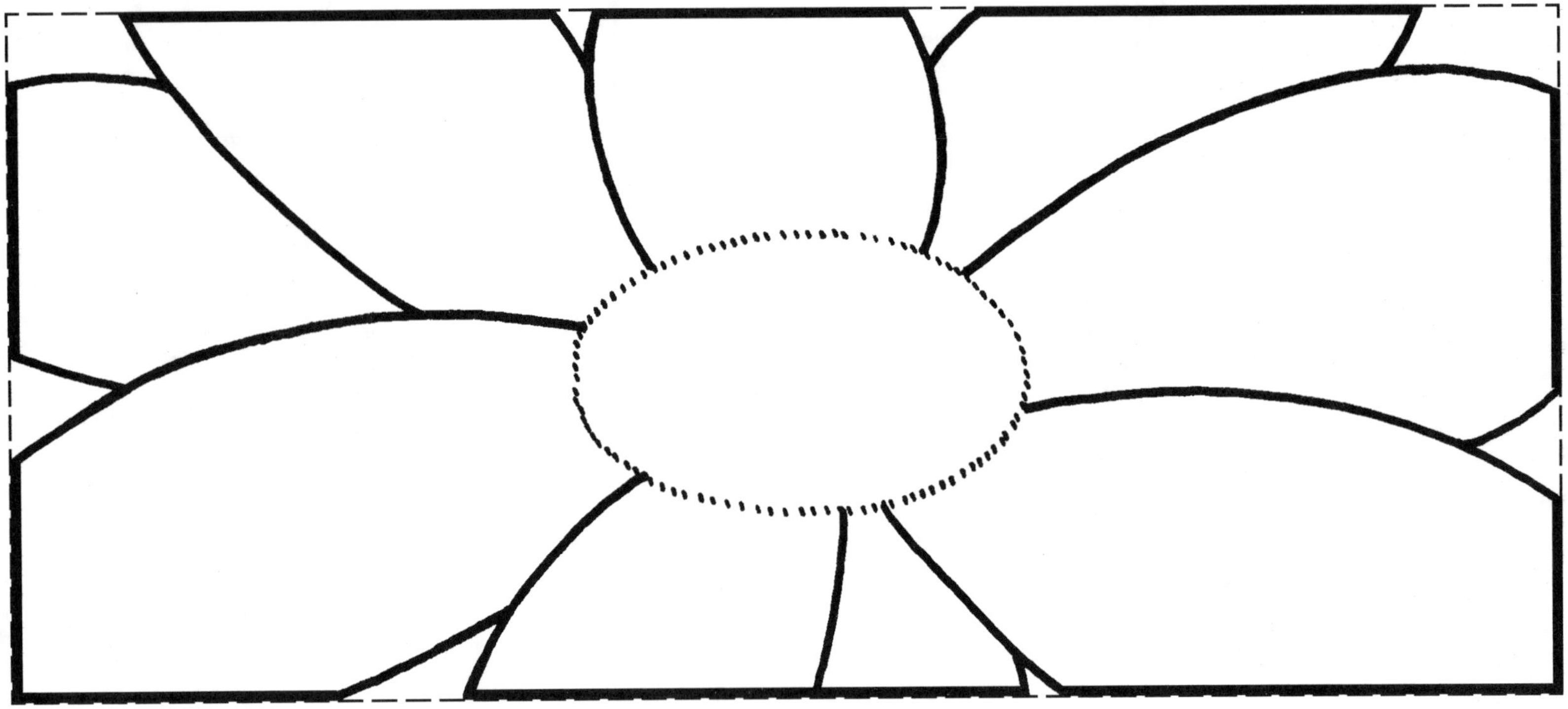

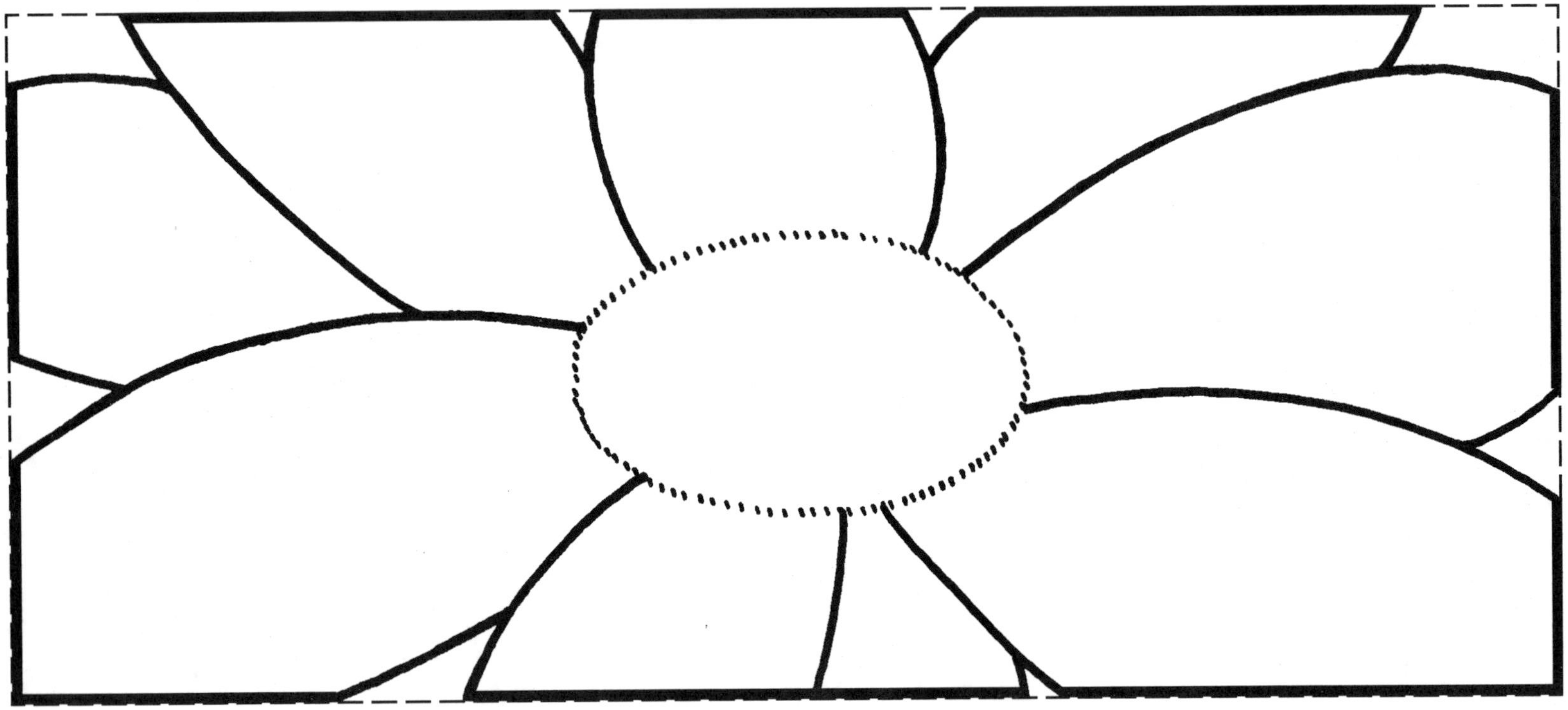

Use to make:
Trifold Books
Trifold Garlands

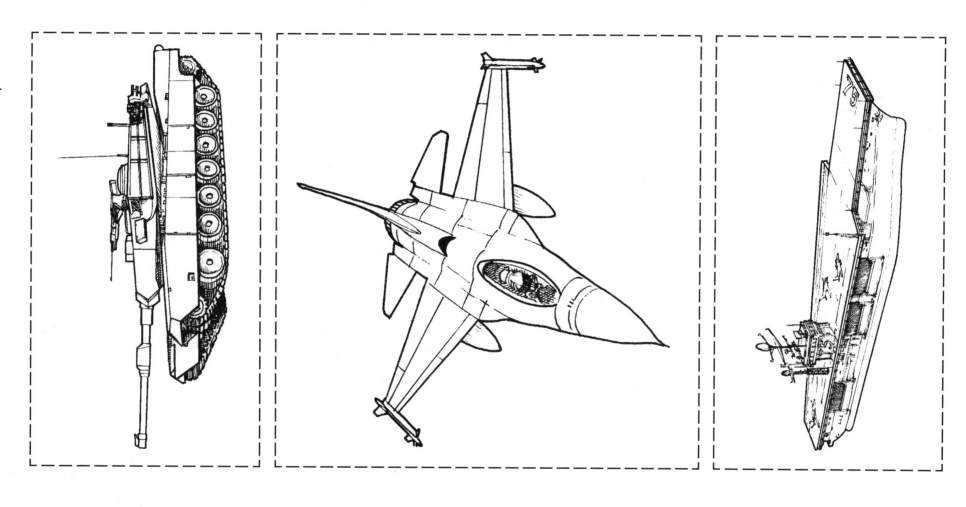

85

Use with Drinking Cup Fold
(see page 56, *Dinah Zike's Big Book of Books and Activities*)
for a Mother's Day bouquet, as a thank you, or as a memorial to a historic figure.

Cinco de Mayo

Use full-page patterns for:
-Desk Top Projects
-Cereal Box Covers
-Large Accordion Books
-Display Cubes
-Giant Ornaments

June

Dairy Month

Father's Day = third Sunday

Flag Day = June 14

Midsummer's Eve

First Day of Summer

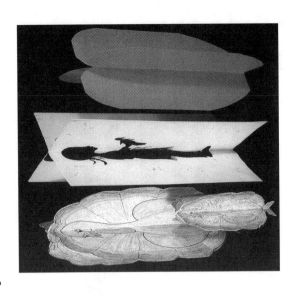

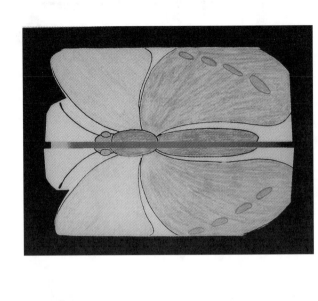

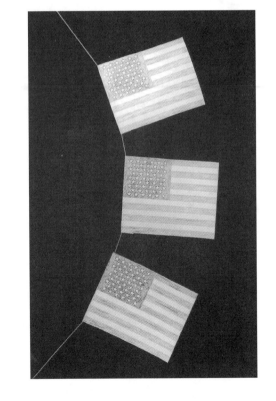

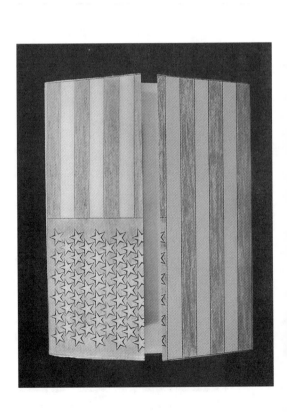

June Birthdays

Use For: Creative Writing Papers; Research Projects; Timelines/Timetables, & Geography Integration

Important Note: It is nearly impossible to verify the actual date of birth of many historic figures. Different sources give differing dates for several birthdays in this list. The birth years listed are more accurate than the birth months or days.

June 1, 1878: John Masefield (English), known as 'the poet of the sea' and author of the poem *Sea-Fever*.
June 2, 1732: Martha Washington, America's first first lady.
June 2, 1840: Thomas Hardy, English architect, author and poet.
June 3, 1808: Jefferson Davis, president of Confederate States.
June 3, 1906: Josephine Baker, Black American vocalist.
June 3, 1904: Dr. Charles R. Drew, American "Father of Blood Plasma".
June 4, 1738: King George III of England.
June 5, 469 B.C.: Socrates, Greek philosopher.
June 6, 1755: Nathan Hale, U.S. patriot.
June 8, 1867: Frank Lloyd Wright, American architect regarded as one of the world's greatest.
June 8, 1810: Robert Schumann, German composer.
June 9, 1781: George Stephenson, British inventor who built first practical locomotive to use steam.
June 9, 1672: Peter the Great, Russian czar.
June 10, 1758: King Kamehameha, unifier of the Hawaiian Islands.
June 10, 1928: Maurice Sendak, American author, *Where the Wild Things Are*.
June 11, 1910: Jacques Cousteau, French oceanographer.
June 12, 1819: Charles Kingsley, English author and clergyman.
June 12, 1929: Anne Frank, German-born, Jewish author of *The Diary of a Young Girl*.
June 12, 1817: Henry David Thoreau, American naturalist and author of *Walden*.
June 13, 1865: William Butler Yeats, Irish poet and dramatist.
June 14, 1906: Margaret Bourke-White, American journalistic photographer.
June 15, 1843: Edward Grieg, Norwegian composer.
June 17, 1703: John Wesley, English minister and founder of Methodism.
June 17, 1818: Charles Gounod, French composer.
June 18, 1850: Cyrus Curtis, American publisher developed magazine publishing into an industry.
June 19, 1623: Blaise Pascal, French philosopher.
June 21, 1850: Daniel Carter Beard, American artist, author and organizer of first U.S. Boy Scout troop.
June 22, 1767: Karl von Humboldt, German naturalist and traveler.
June 22, 1907: Anne Morrow Lindbergh, American author and wife of Charles Lindbergh.
June 24, 1813: Henry Ward Beecher, American preacher, lecturer, and brother of Harriett Beecher Stowe.
June 26, 1892: Pearl S. Buck, American novelist who lived many years in China.
June 27, 1880: Helen Keller, blind and deaf American author and lecturer.
June 27, 1872: Paul Laurence Dunbar, Black American poet.
June 28, 1491: King Henry VIII of England.
June 28, 1577: Peter Paul Rubens, Flemish painter.
June 28, 1712: Jean Jacques Rousseau, French philosopher and political theorist for French Revolution.
June 28, 1703: John Wesley, English evangelist and founder of Methodism.
June 29, 1900: Antoine de Saint-Exupery, French aviator and author of *The Little Prince*.
June 29, 1858: George Goethals, American civil engineer and supervisor of Panama Canal construction.

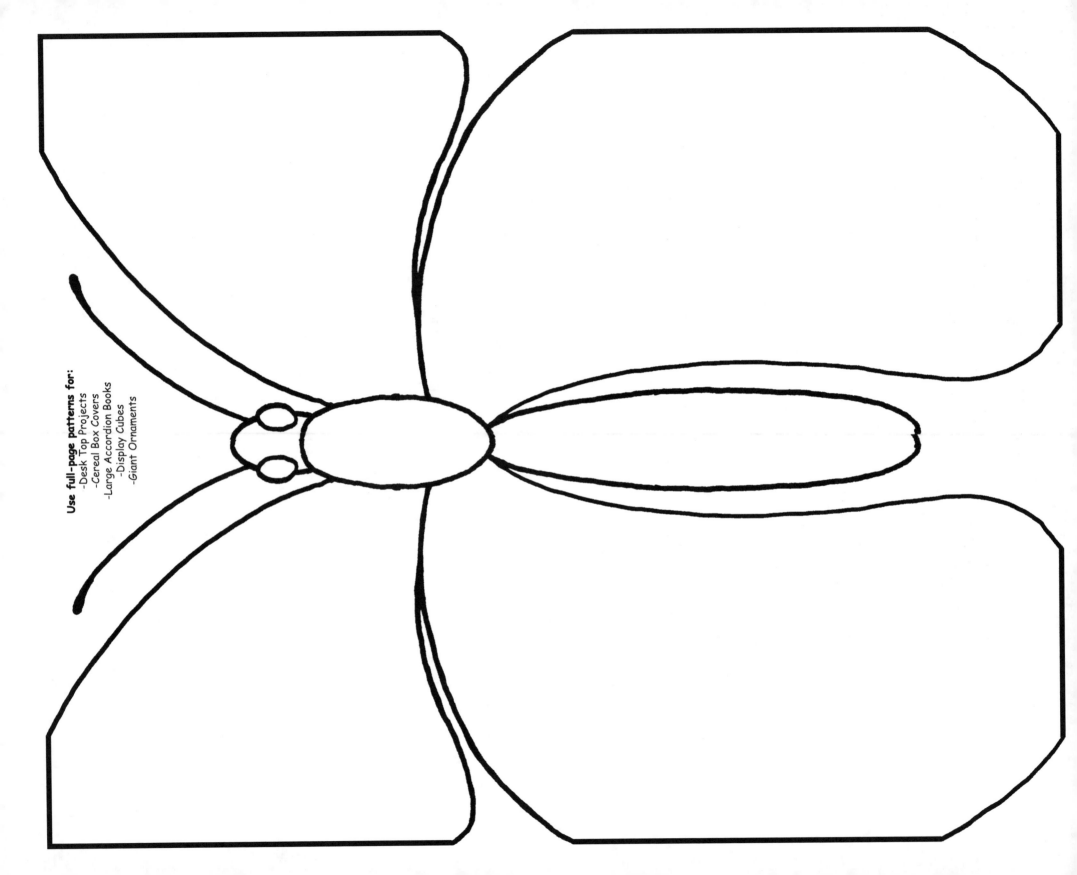

Use full-page patterns for:
-Desk Top Projects
-Cereal Box Covers
-Large Accordion Books
-Display Cubes
-Giant Ornaments

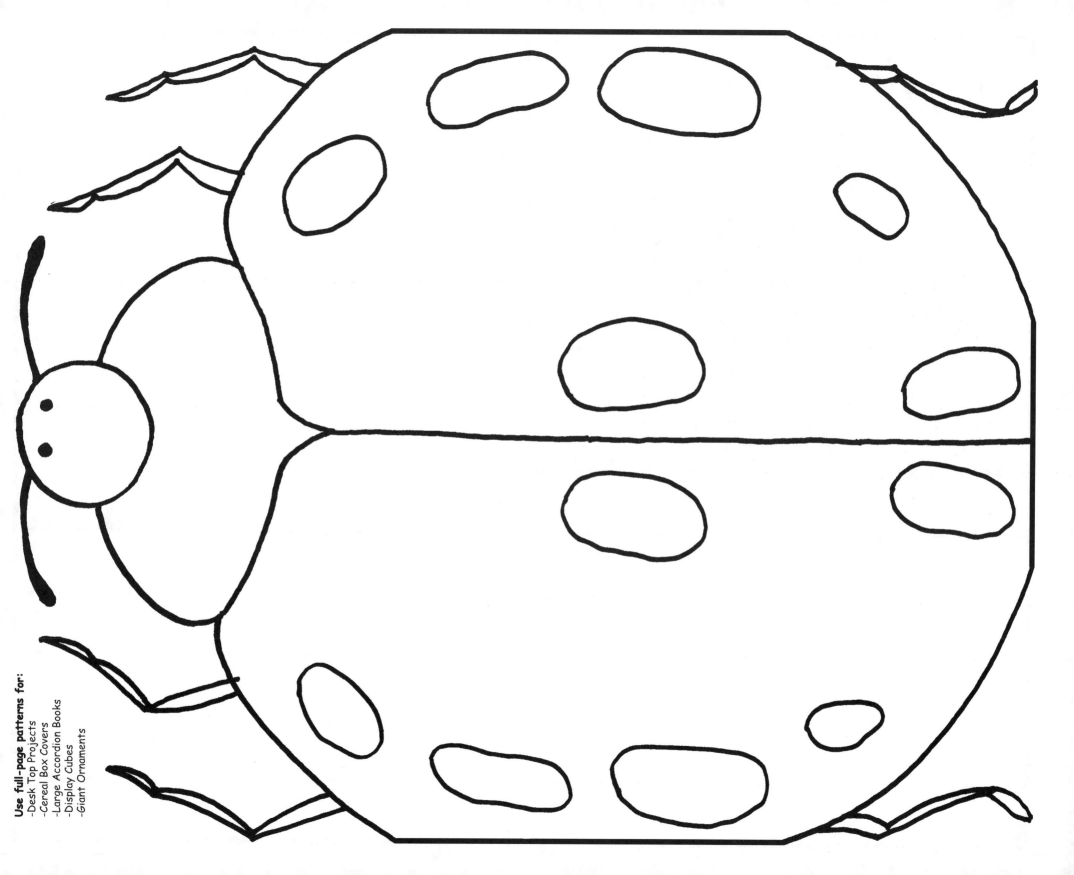

Wrap cut-out flags around a straw and glue them together to make a miniature American flag.

Use small butterflies for:
Garland Patterns
Pop-up pictures
Small 2-D or 3-D Ornaments
Milk Box Covers
Cutout lids for Display Box

Use medium-sized butterflies for:
Picture Frame Books
Large 2-D or 3-D ornaments

Father's Day: Choose A Tie

1. Make a shutter fold using a piece of 11" X 17" paper.
2. As illustrated, fold the top of the shutter fold to look like a collar.
3. Fold the tie in half like a hotdog, and cut the tie in half along the fold line.
4. Glue the two pieces on either side of the shutterfold opening.
   Use this as a writing project for Father's Day.

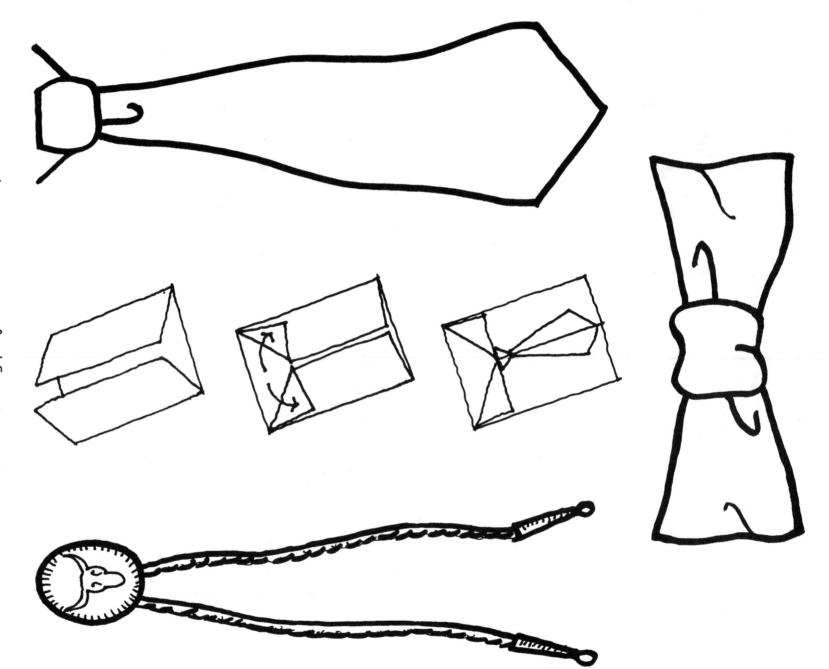

July

July 4: Fourth of July or Independence Day
(Americans celebrate independence from England.)

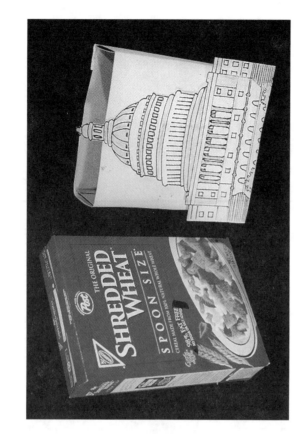

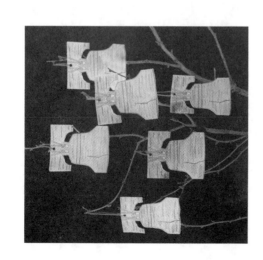

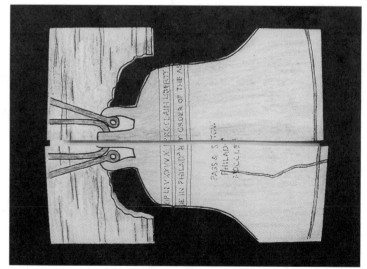

July Birthdays

Important Note: It is nearly impossible to verify the actual date of birth of many historic figures. Different sources give differing dates for several birthdays in this list. The birth years listed are more accurate than the birth months or days.

July 4, 1872: Calvin Coolidge, 30th U. S. President.
July 4, 1901: Louis Armstrong, American jazz musician.
July 4, 1918: Ann Landers and Abigail Van Buren, American twins and newspaper advice columnists.
July 4, 1804: Nathaniel Hawthorne, American novelist (*The Scarlet Letter*) and short-story writer.
July 5, 1709: Etienne de Silhouette, French politician who cut out shadow portraits.
July 5, 1810: P. T. Barnum, American showman and founder of "*The Greatest Show on Earth.*"
July 6, 1886: Beatrix Potter, English author and illustrator, creator of Peter Rabbit.
July 7, 1887: Marc Chagall, Russian Jewish artist.
July 8, 1839: John D. Rockefeller, American industrialist and philanthropist.
July 10, 1834: James McNeill Whistler, American painter and etcher.
July 11, 1767: John Quincy Adams, 6th U. S. President.
July 11, 1899: E.B. White, American author of *Charlotte's Web.*
July 12, 100 B.C.: Julius Caesar was born.
July 12, 1817: Henry David Thoreau, American writer and naturalist.
July 12, 1864: George Washing Carver, Black American botanist, educator, and inventor.
July 12, 1895: Buckminster Fuller, American architect, inventor, designer.
July 12, 1913: Jesse Owens, Black American track and field athletic champion.
July 14, 1904: Isaac Bashevis Singer, Jewish storyteller and novelist.
July 14, 1918: Ingmar Bergman, Swedish filmmaker.
July 15, 1606: Rembrandt Harmenszoon van Rijn, Dutch painter.
July 18, 1921: John Glenn, U.S. astronaut and senator.
July 21, 1899: Ernest Hemingway, American writer.
July 22, 1849: Emma Lazarus, Jewish-American poet. Wrote sonnet inscribed on the Statue of Liberty.
July 24, 1783: Simon Bolivar, South American explorer and liberator.
July 24, 1898: Amelia Earhart, American aviator and first woman to fly across the Atlantic.
July 24, 1802: Alexandre Dumas, French novelist and author of *The Three Musketeers.*
July 26, 1875: Carl Jung, Swiss psychoanalytic visionary.
July 26, 1892: Pearl S. Buck, American author.
July 26, 1856: George Bernard Shaw, British playwright, novelist, and critic.
July 29, 1887: Marcel Duchamp, French-American artist.
July 30, 1818: Emily Bronte, English author of *Wuthering Heights.*
July 30, 1863: Henry Ford, American automobile inventor.
July 30, 1898: Henry Moore, British sculptor.

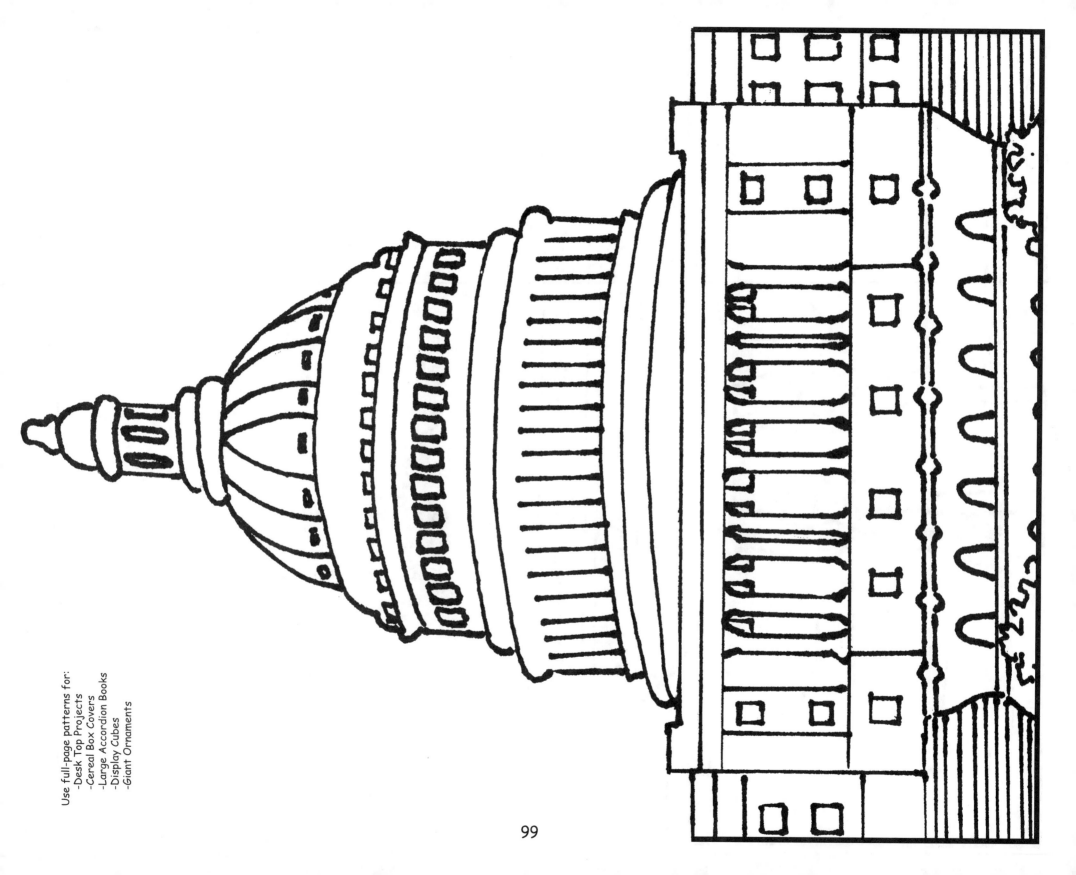

Use full-page patterns for:
-Desk Top Projects
-Cereal Box Covers
-Large Accordion Books
-Display Cubes
-Giant Ornaments

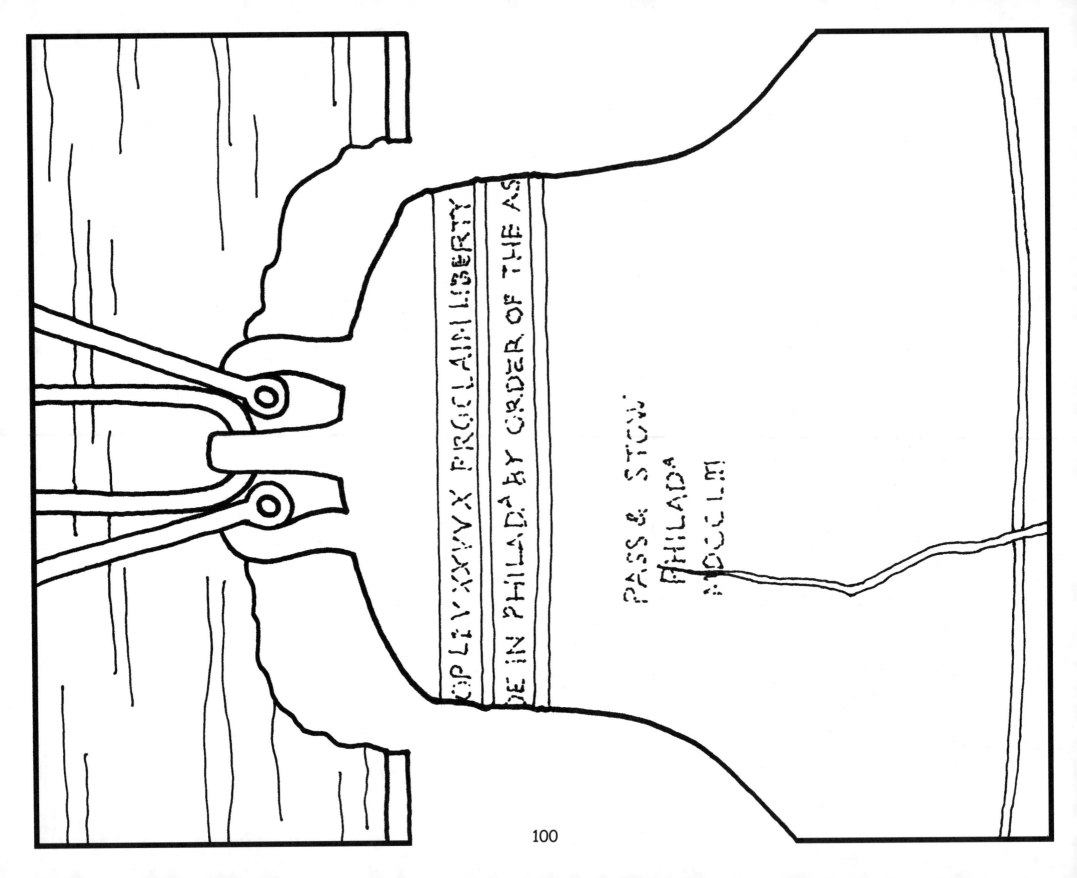

100

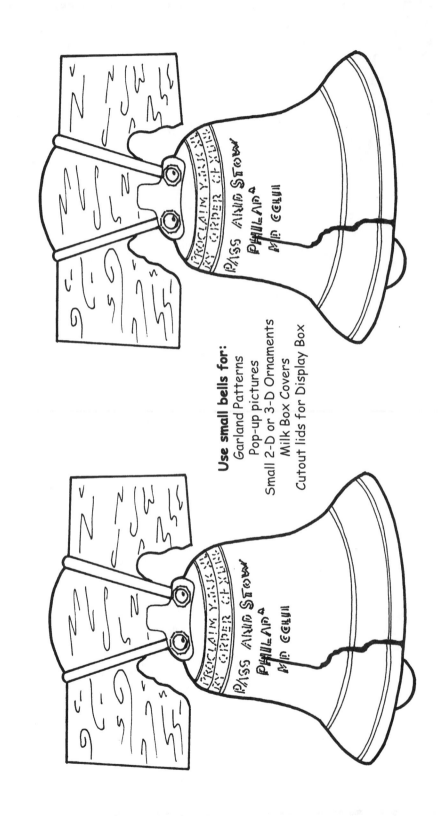

Use medium-sized bells for:
Picture Frame Books
Large 2-D or 3-D ornaments

Use small bells for:
Garland Patterns
Pop-up pictures
Small 2-D or 3-D Ornaments
Milk Box Covers
Cutout lids for Display Box

102

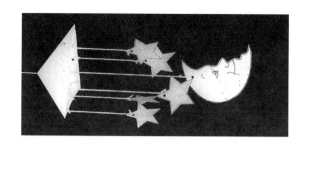

August

August 2 = Friendship Day

August 19 = National Aviation Day

August 25 = UFO Day

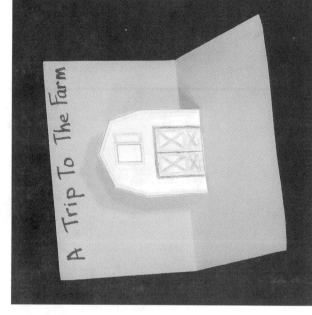

A Trip To The Farm

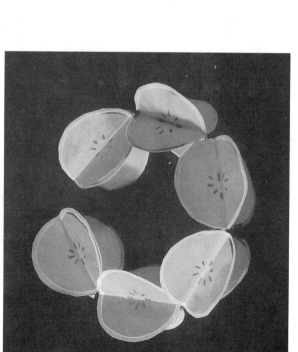

August Birthdays

Use For: Creative Writing Papers; Research Projects; Timelines/Timetables, & Geography Integration

Important Note: It is nearly impossible to verify the actual date of birth of many historic figures. Different sources give differing dates for several birthdays in this list. The birth years listed are more accurate than the birth months or days.

August 1, 1819: Herman Melville, American author of *Moby Dick*.

August 4, 1792: Percy Bysshe Shelley, English poet.

August 6, 1809: Alfred Lord Tennyson, English poet of the Victorian age.

August 7, 1904: Ralph Bunche, Black American educator and statesman.

August 8, 1896: Marjorie Kinnan Rawlings, American author of *The Yearling*.

August 9, 1896: Jean Piaget, Swiss psychologist and child behaviorist.

August 10, 1874: Herbert Hoover, 31st U.S. President.

August 11, 1921: Alex Haley, Black American author of *Roots*.

August 12, 1859: Katherine Lee Bates, American poet and songwriter of *America the Beautiful*.

August 13, 1422: William Caxton, the first English printer of the first book printed in English.

August 13, 1860: Annie Oakley, American rifle sharpshooter.

August 13, 1899: Alfred Hitchcock, American film director.

August 15, 1771: Sir Walter Scott, Scottish poet and first historical novelist.

August 17, 1786: Davy Crockett, American frontiersman.

August 18, 1587: Virginia Dare, first English child born in America.

August 18, 1774: Meriwether Lewis, American explorer and leader of Lewis and Clark Expedition.

August 20, 1833: Benjamin Harrison, 23rd U. S. President.

August 20, 1881: Edgar A. Guest, American poet--"It takes a heap o'living to make a house a home."

August 22, 1893: Dorothy Parker, American writer and humorist.

August 24, 1899: Jorge Luis Borges, Argentine author.

August 25, 1836: Francis Bret Harte, American writer about life in the American West.

August 26, 1867: Robert Russa Moton, Black American educator who succeeded Booker T. Washington.

August 27, 551 B.C.: Confucius, Chinese philosopher and writer.

August 27, 1908: Lyndon B. Johnson, 36th U. S. President.

August 28, 1749: Johann Goethe, German poet.

August 29, 1632: John Locke, English philosopher and educational theorist.

August 29, 1809: Oliver Wendell Holmes, American poet, physician, and essayist.

August 30, 1797: Mary Wollstonecraft Shelley, English author of *Frankenstein*.

August 30, 1870: Maria Montessore, Italian educator and founder of schools.

August 31, 12 A.D.: Caligula, Roman emperor.

August 31, 1943: R. Crumb, American cartoonist.

August 31, 1908: William Saroyan, Armenian-American author.

August 31, 1628: John Bunyan, British preacher and author of *Pilgrim's Progress*.

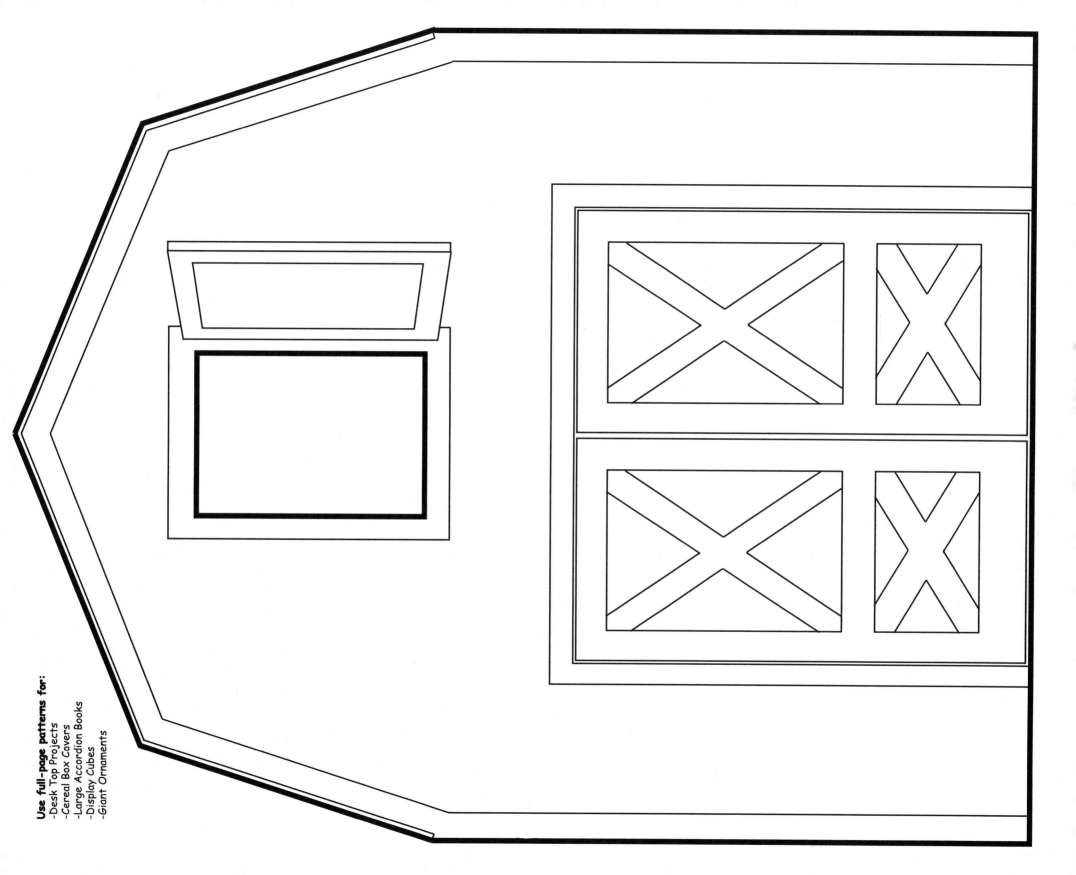

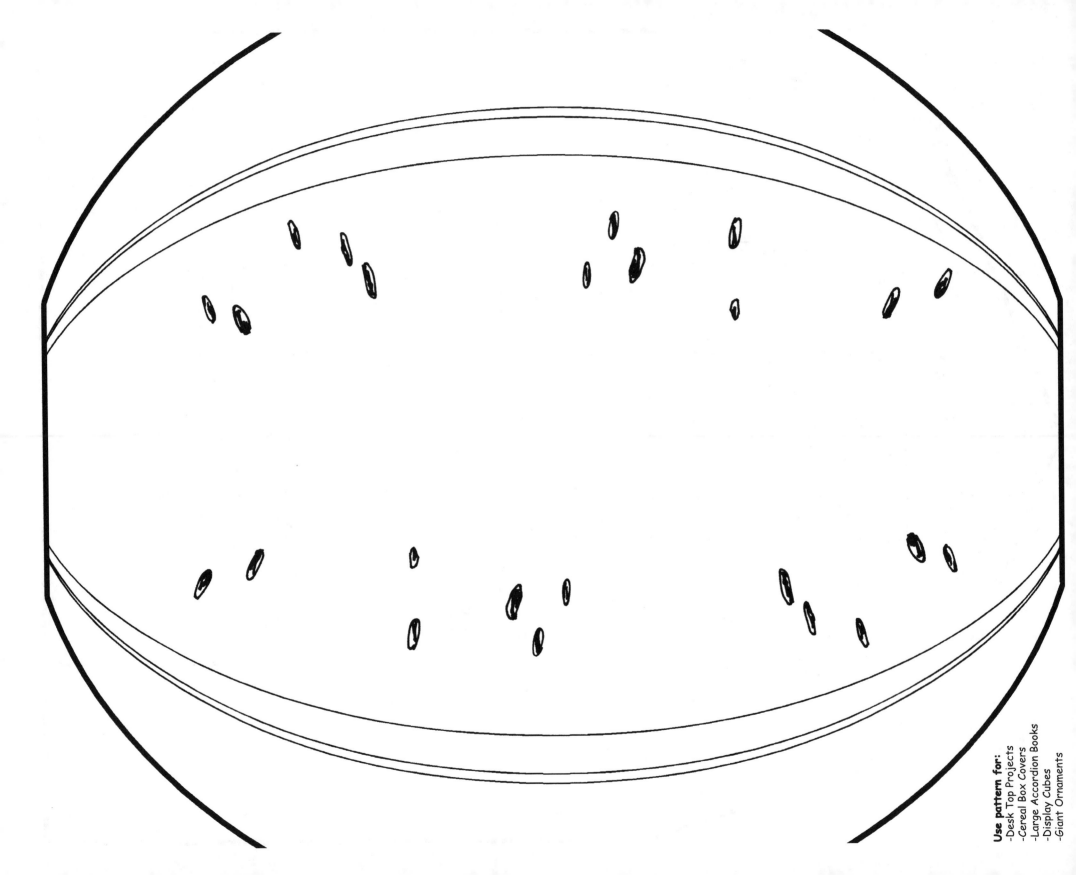

Use For:
2-D ornaments
Summer Night Sky Mobiles
Display Box Lid Cutouts
Christmas Decorations
Star Reports or vocabulary words
Moon Reports or vocabulary words

107

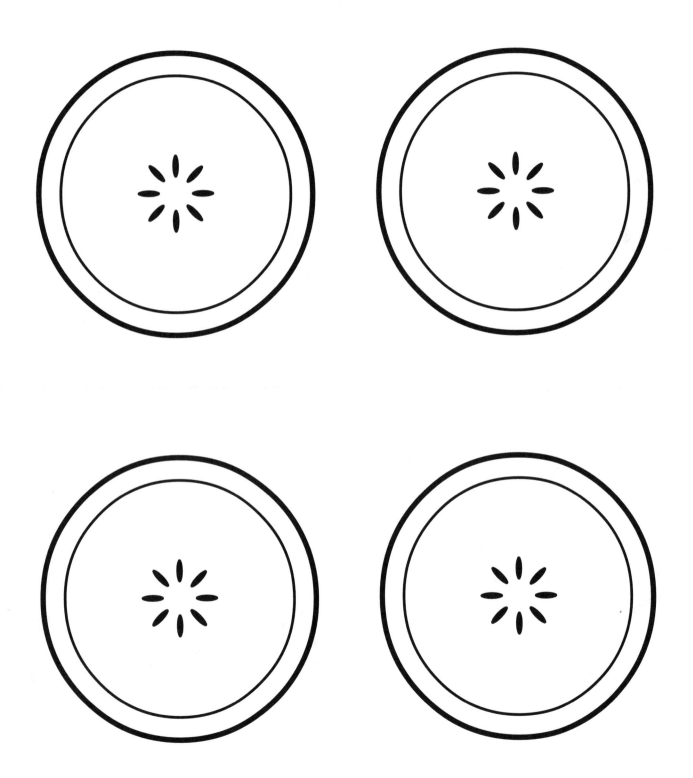

Use to make watermelon mobiles.

1. Cut the large circle out of green construction paper.
2. Cut the inner, smaller circle out of red construction paper.
3. Center the smaller circle on top of the larger one and glue it in place.
4. Punch a hole on the edge and hang from a mobile.

Investigate the history of watermelons.
What % of the fruit is water?
List the steps to growing a watermelon plant.
How are watermelons shipped?
Where are they grown?

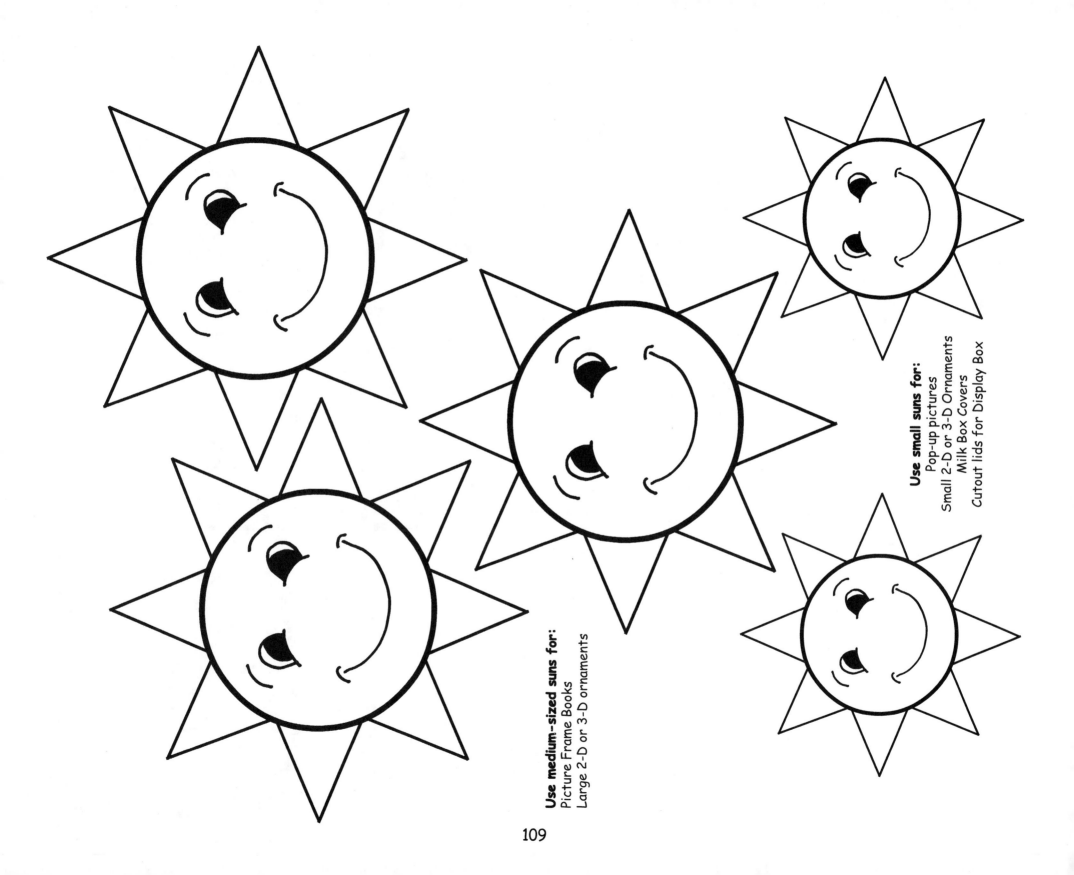

Use small suns for:
Pop-up pictures
Small 2-D or 3-D Ornaments
Milk Box Covers
Cutout lids for Display Box

Use medium-sized suns for:
Picture Frame Books
Large 2-D or 3-D ornaments

September

Labor Day = first Monday of September

Grandparent's Day = first Sunday after Labor Day

Hispanic Heritage Week = begins the second Sunday

National Dog Week = begins the Sunday of the last full week

Rosh Hashana = celebration of Jewish New Year
(occurs in September or October)

American Indian Day = September 26 or fourth Friday

Citizenship Day = September 17
(adoption of Constitution)

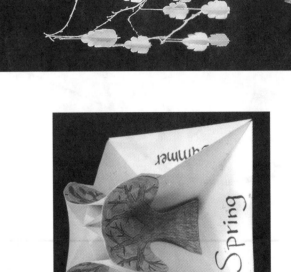

September Birthdays

Use For: Creative Writing Papers; Research Projects: Timelines/Timetables, & Geography Integration

Important Note: It is nearly impossible to verify the actual date of birth of many historic figures. Different sources give differing dates for several birthdays in this list. The birth years listed are more accurate than the birth months or days.

September 2, 1850: Eugene Field, American journalist and author called "the poet of childhood."

September 3, 1856: Louis Henri Sullivan, American Architect.

September 4, 518 B.C.: Pindar, Greek choral lyricist.

September 4, 1802: Marcus Whitman, American pioneer, doctor, and missionary to Native Americans.

September 5, 1847: Jessie James, American outlaw.

September 5, 1638: Louis XIV, king of France.

September 7, 1533: Queen Elizabeth I of England's birthday is honored.

September 6, 1860: Jane Addams, American pioneer social worker.

September 8, 1157: Richard the Lionhearted, Crusader and King of England.

September 9, 1027: William the Conqueror, King of England.

September 9, 1828: Leo Tolstoy, Russian novelist.

September 10, 1892: Arthur Compton, American scientist in the field of X rays and cosmic rays.

September 11, 1826: O. Henry (William S. Porter) American author of short stories.

September 13, 1916: Roald Dahl, Welsh author of *James and the Giant Peach.*

September 13, 1900: Walter Reed, American army surgeon.

September 14, 1769: Alexander von Humboldt, German naturalist.

September 14, 1934: Kate Millett, American feminist.

September 15, 1789: James Fenimore Cooper, American novelist, author of *The Last of the Mohicans.*

September 16, 1518: Tintoretto (Jacopo Robusti), Italian painter.

September 18, 1709: Samuel Johnson, English writer and dictionary-maker (lexicographer).

September 18, 1905: Greta Garbo, Swedish-American movie star.

September 20, 356 B.C.: Alexander the Great, king of Macedonia and military leader.

September 21, 1866: H.G. Wells, English author noted for science-fiction and political philosophy.

September 22 or 23, 63 B.C.: Augustus Caesar, first emperor of the Roman Empire.

September 23, 1932: Ray Charles, Black American singer/musician who lost his sight as a child.

September 23, 1949: Bruce Springsteen, American rock-and-roll singer and song writer.

September 23, 1952: Dinah Zike, Texas-born educational author of this book.

September 25, 1906: Dmitri Shostakovich, Russian composer.

September 25, 1897: William Faulkner, American novelist and short story writer.

September 26, 1775: Johnny Appleseed [John Chapman], American pioneer and nurseryman.

September 26, 1898: George Gershwin, American composer of popular songs and musicals.

September 26, 1888: T.S. Eliot, Nobel Prize winning, American-born English poet and playwright.

September 27, 1722: Samuel Adams, American patriot and leader of the Boston Tea Party.

September 27, 1840: Thomas Nast, German-born American cartoonist for Harper's Weekly.

September 29, 1758: Horatio Nelson, British admiral and naval hero who helped Britain rule the seas.

September 30, 1928: Elie Wiesel, Jewish French-American writer and Nobel Peace Prize winner.

September 12, 1913: Jesse Owens, Olympic gold metal winning Black American athlete.

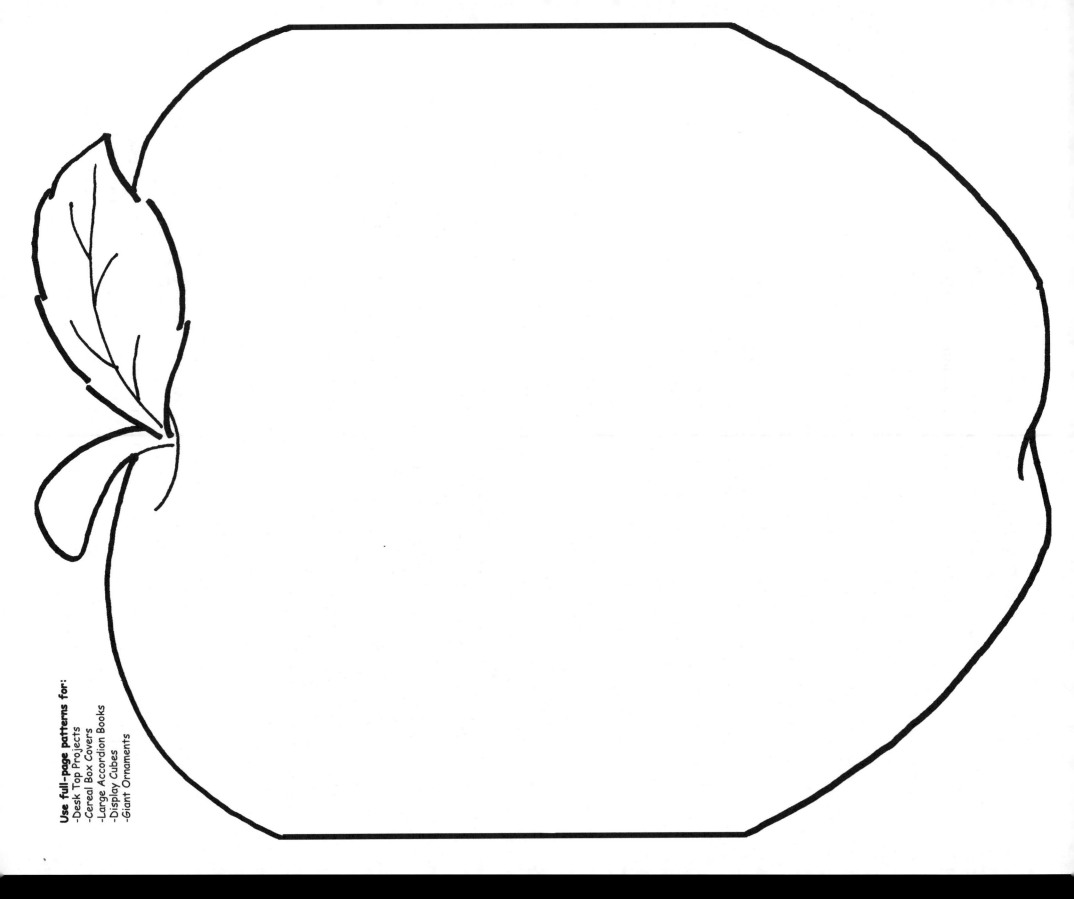

Use full-page patterns for:
-Desk Top Projects
-Cereal Box Covers
-Large Accordion Books
-Display Cubes
-Giant Ornaments

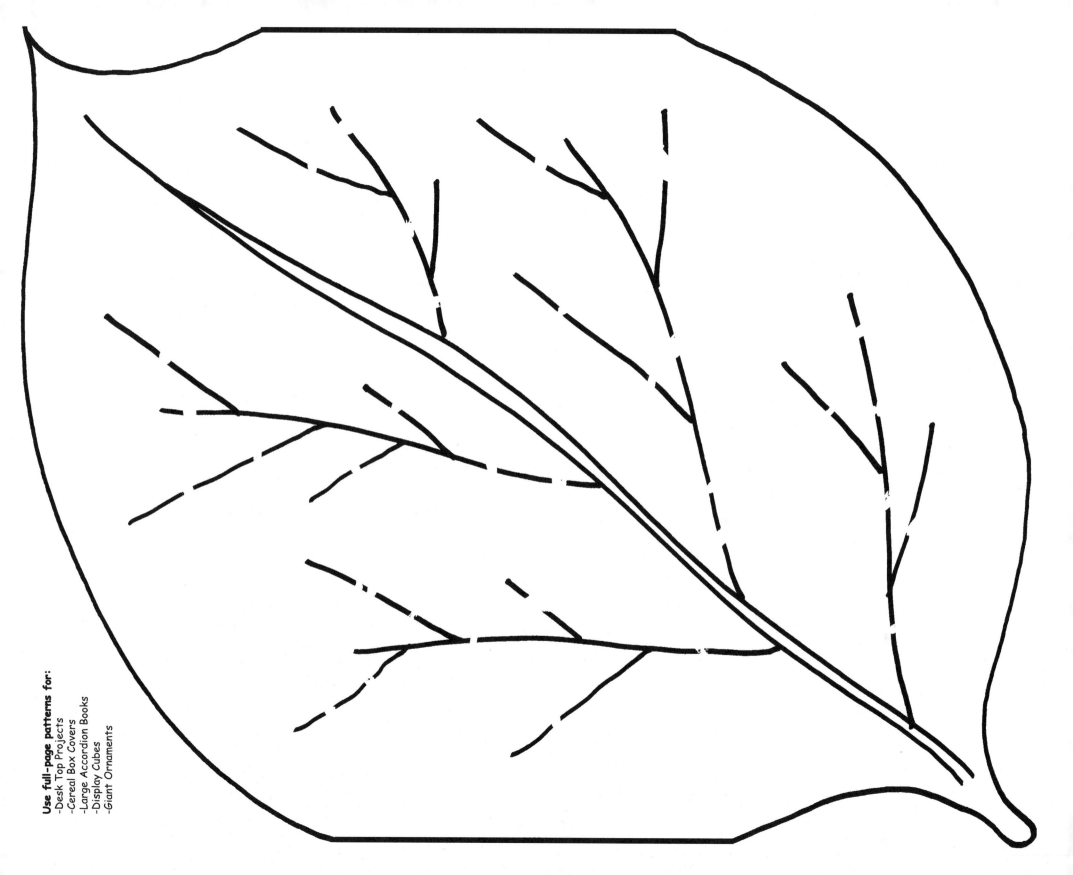

Use full-page patterns for:
-Desk Top Projects
-Cereal Box Covers
-Large Accordion Books
-Display Cubes
-Giant Ornaments

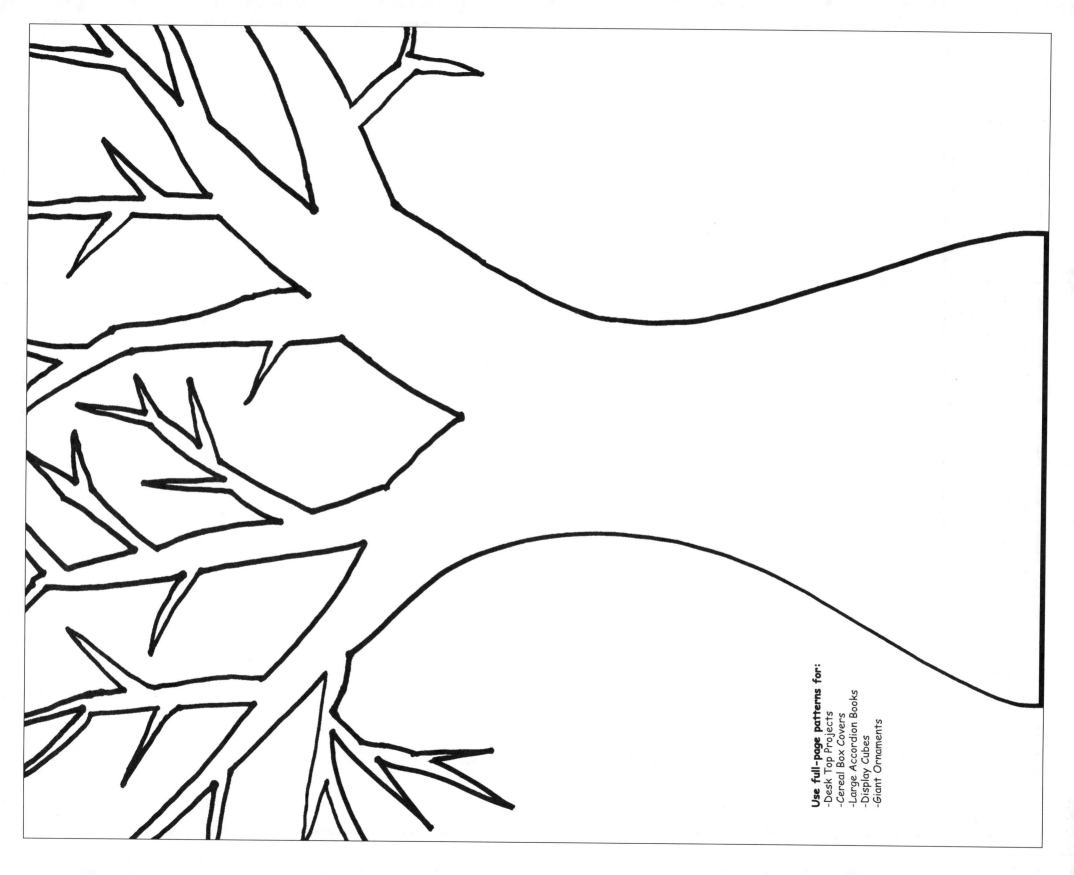

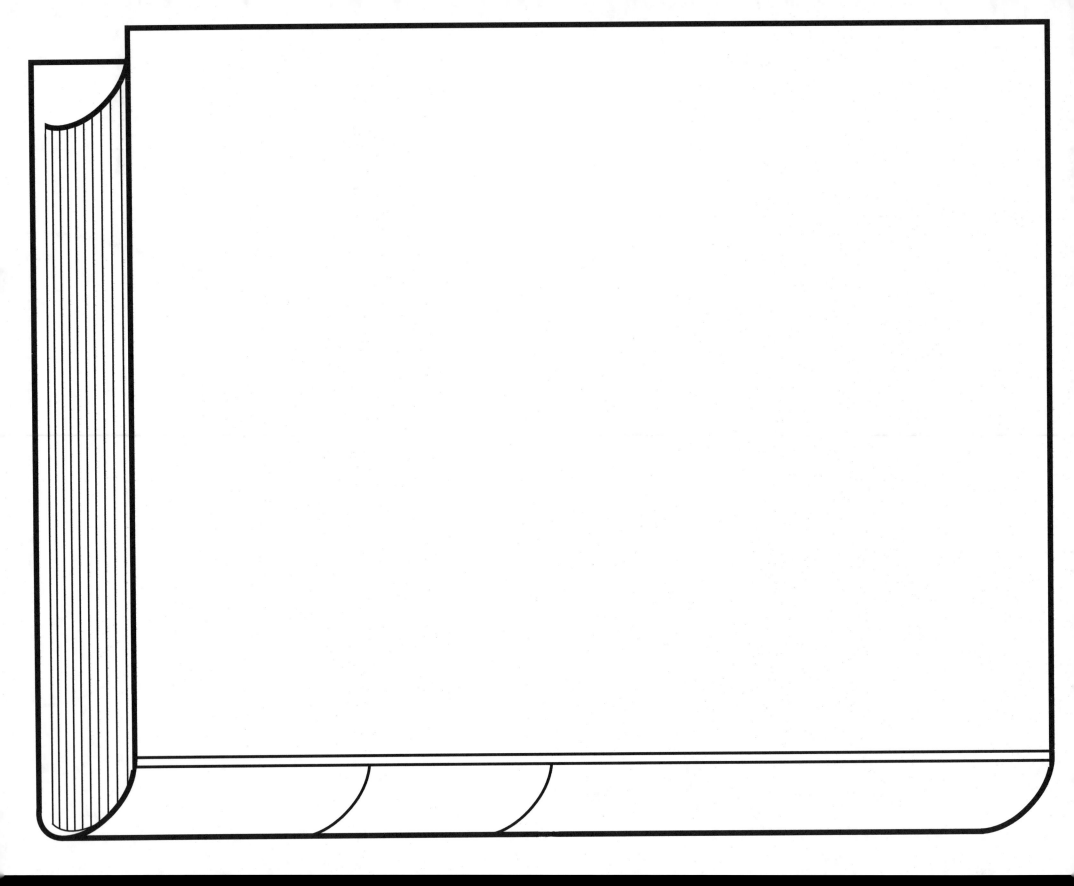

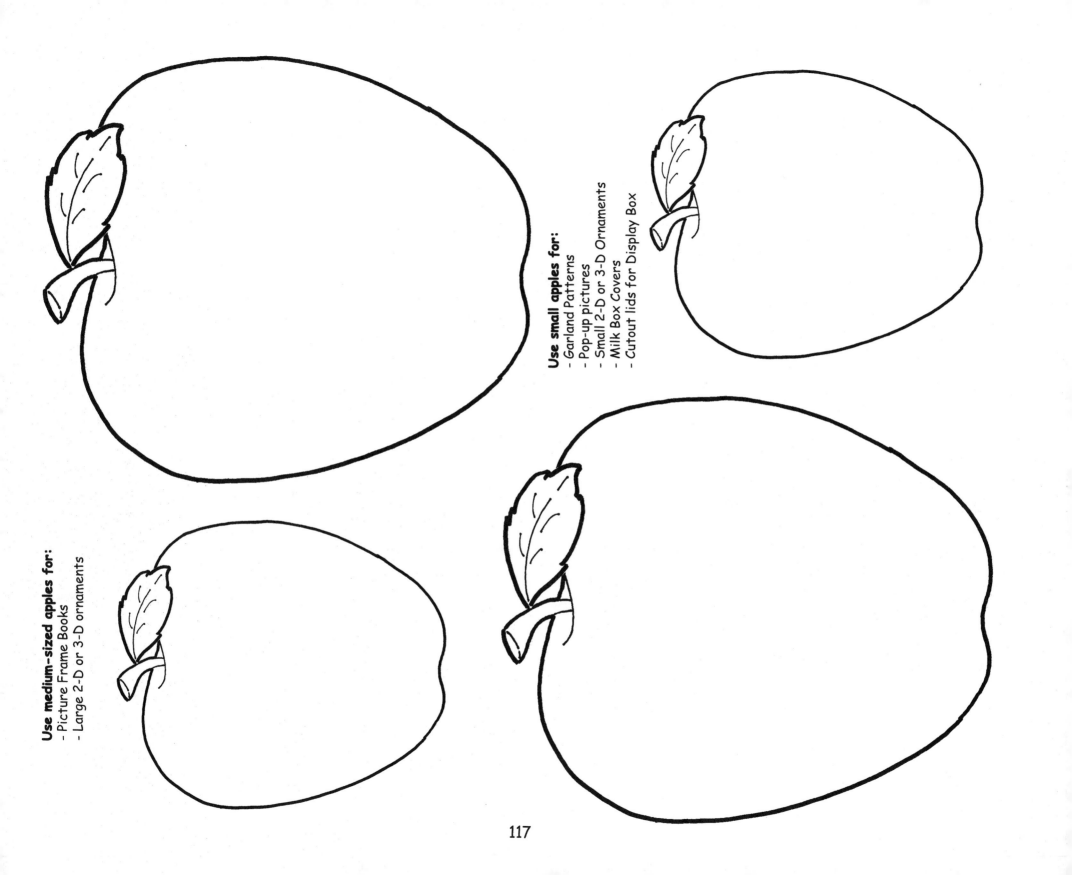

Use small apples for:
- Garland Patterns
- Pop-up pictures
- Small 2-D or 3-D Ornaments
- Milk Box Covers
- Cutout lids for Display Box

Use medium-sized apples for:
- Picture Frame Books
- Large 2-D or 3-D ornaments

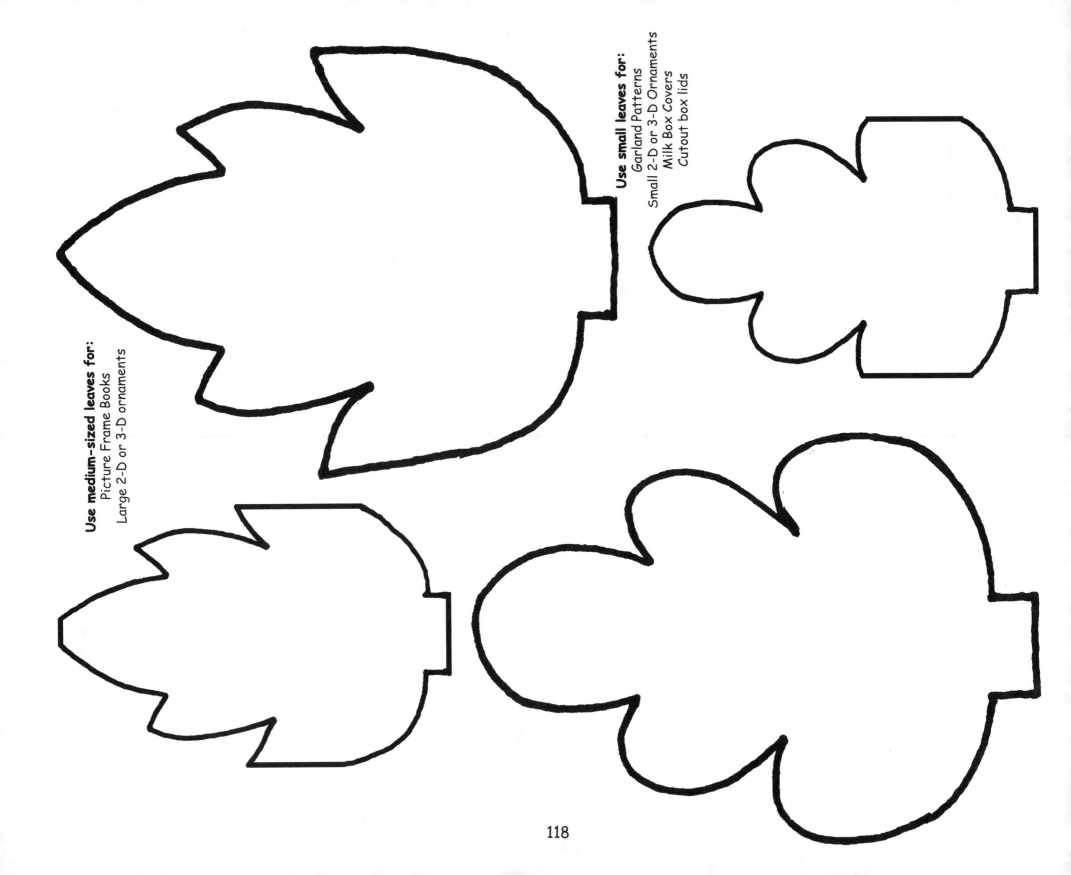

Use small leaves for:
Garland Patterns
Small 2-D or 3-D Ornaments
Milk Box Covers
Cutout box lids

Use medium-sized leaves for:
Picture Frame Books
Large 2-D or 3-D ornaments

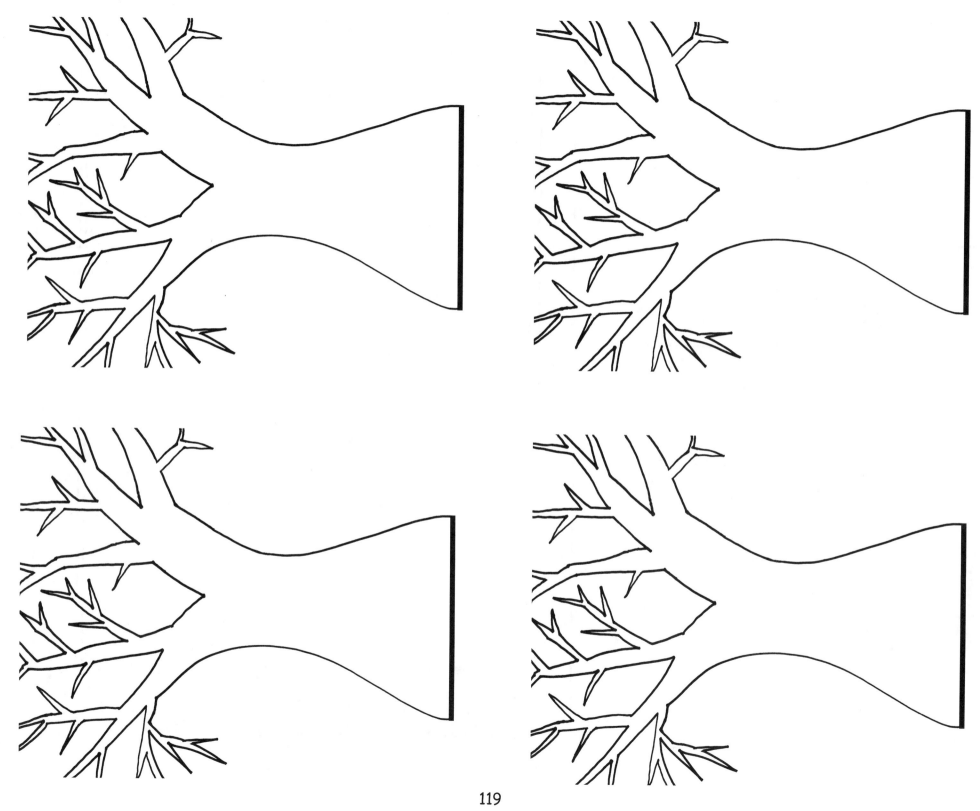

Book Banners: To record titles and reviews of books read by a class or student.

October

National Newspaper Week = begins the first or second Sunday

Fire Prevention Week = during the week of October 8

National Forest Products Week = begins the third Sunday

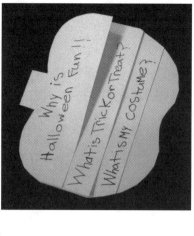

Columbus Day = second Monday

Child Health Day = October 3

Lief Erickson Day = October 9

Poetry Day = October 15

World Food Day = October 16

Alaska Day = October 18

Halloween and All Saints Day = October 31

UNICEF (United Nations Children's Fund) Day = October 31

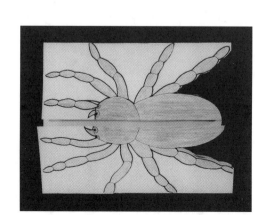

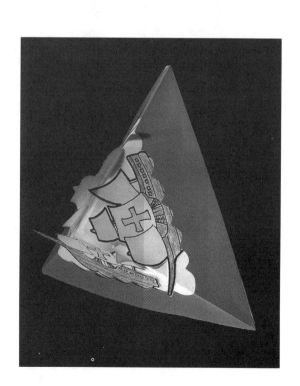

October Birthdays

Use For: Creative Writing Papers; Research Projects; Timelines/Timetables, & Geography Integration

Important Note: It is nearly impossible to verify the actual date of birth of many historic figures. Different sources give differing dates for several birthdays in this list. The birth years listed are more accurate than the birth months or days.

October 1, 1924:   James Earl (Jimmy) Carter, 39th U.S. President.

October 2, 1869:   Mohandas Gandhi, Hindu Nationalist leader and a pacifist.

October 4, 1822:   Rutherford B. Hayes, 19th U.S. President.

October 4, 1182:   Saint Francis of Assisi, Italian friar and founder of the Franciscans.

October 5, 1829:   Chester A. Arthur, 21st U.S. President.

October 9, 1835:   Camille Saint-Saens, French composer.

October 9, 1547:   Miguel de Cervantes, Spanish author of *Don Quixote*.

October 10, 1813: Guiseppe Verdi, Italian composer.

October 11, 1884: Eleanor Roosevelt, U.S. first lady, diplomat, and humanitarian.

October 13, 1754: Molly Pitcher, American Revolutionary War heroine.

October 14, 1644: William Penn, founder of the state of Pennsylvania.

October 14, 1894: e.e. cummings, American poet.

October 14, 1890: Dwight D. Eisenhower, 34th U. S. President.

October 15, 70 B.C.: Virgil, Roman poet and the reason for Poetry Day on this date.

October 16, 1758: Noah Webster, American educator, scholar, and compiler of *Webster's Dictionary*.

October 16, 1854: Oscar Wilde, Irish novelist, playwright, poet.

October 17, 1915: Arthur Miller, American dramatist who wrote *Death of a Salesman*.

October 18, 1830: Helen Hunt Jackson, American author and poet who worked with Native Americans.

October 19, 1735: John Adams, 2nd U. S. President.

October 20, 1632: Sir Christopher Wren, English architect.

October 21, 1760: Katsushuka Hokusai, Japanese artist.

October 21, 1833: Alfred Nobel, Swedish inventor of dynamite who established the Nobel Prizes.

October 21, 1772: Samuel Taylor Coleridge, English poet, wrote *The Rime of the Ancient Mariner*.

October 22, 1811: Franz Liszt, Hungarian composer and piano virtuoso.

October 25, 1825: Johann Strauss Jr., Austrian composer.

October 25, 1881: Pablo Picasso, prolific Spanish painter and sculptor.

October 25, 1888: Adm. Richard E. Byrd, American author, aviator, and Polar explorer.

October 27, 1858: Theodore Roosevelt, 26th U. S. President.

October 27, 1914: Dylan Thomas, Welsh poet.

October 27, 1728: Captain James Cook, British explorer and navigator.

October 28, 1466: Desiderius Erasmus, Dutch scholar known for statement, "Time reveals all things."

October 31, 1795: John Keats, English poet trained to be in medicine.

October 31, 1632: Jan Vermeer, Dutch painter.

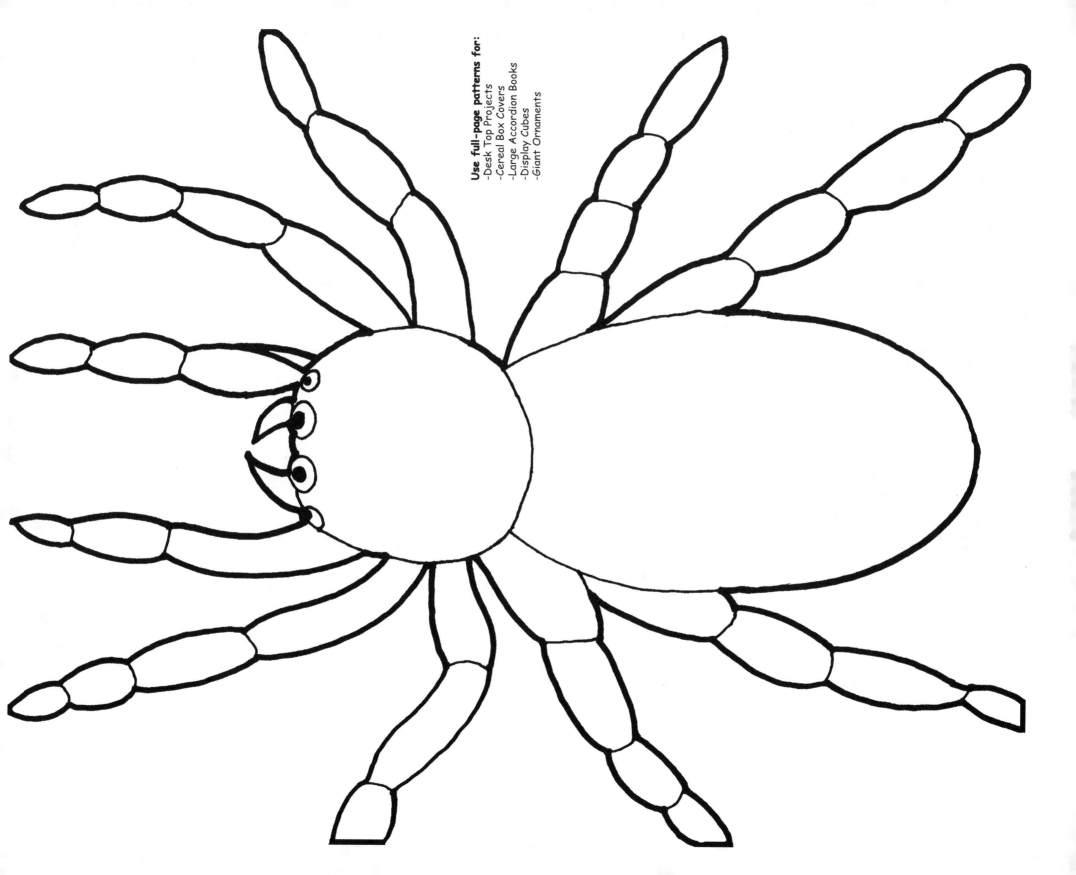

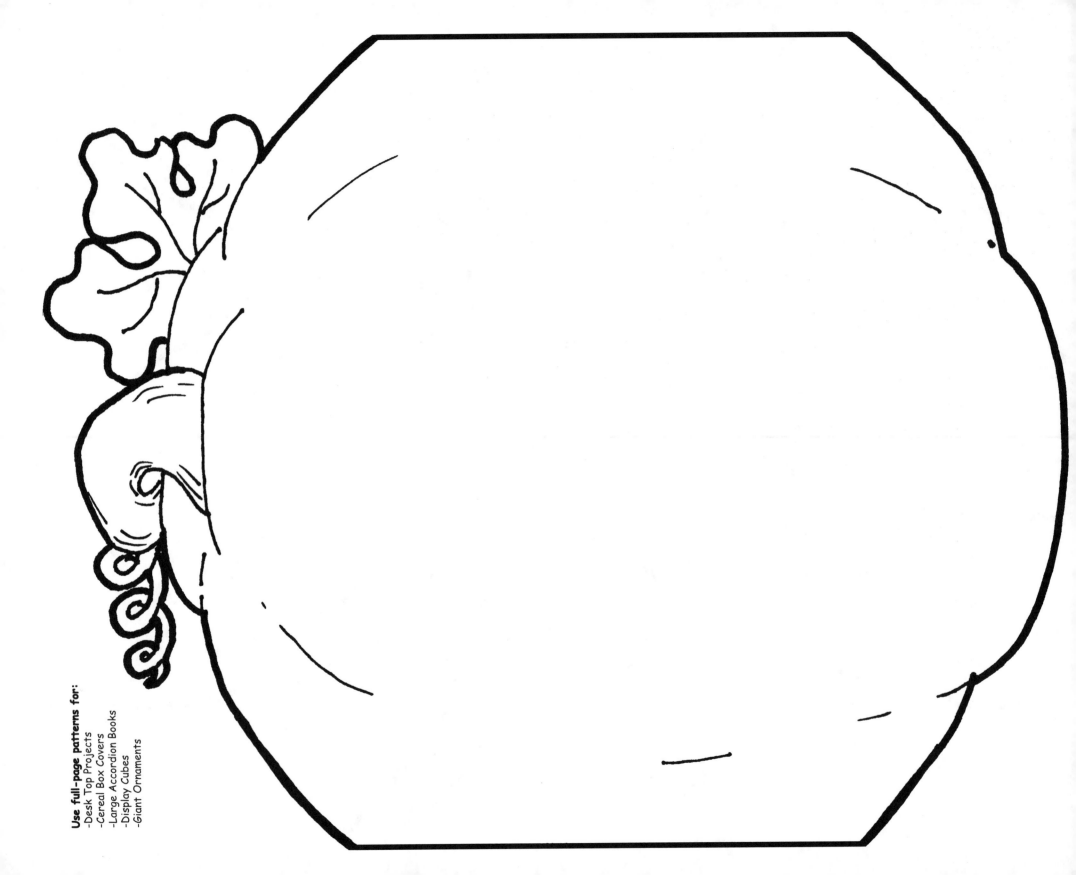

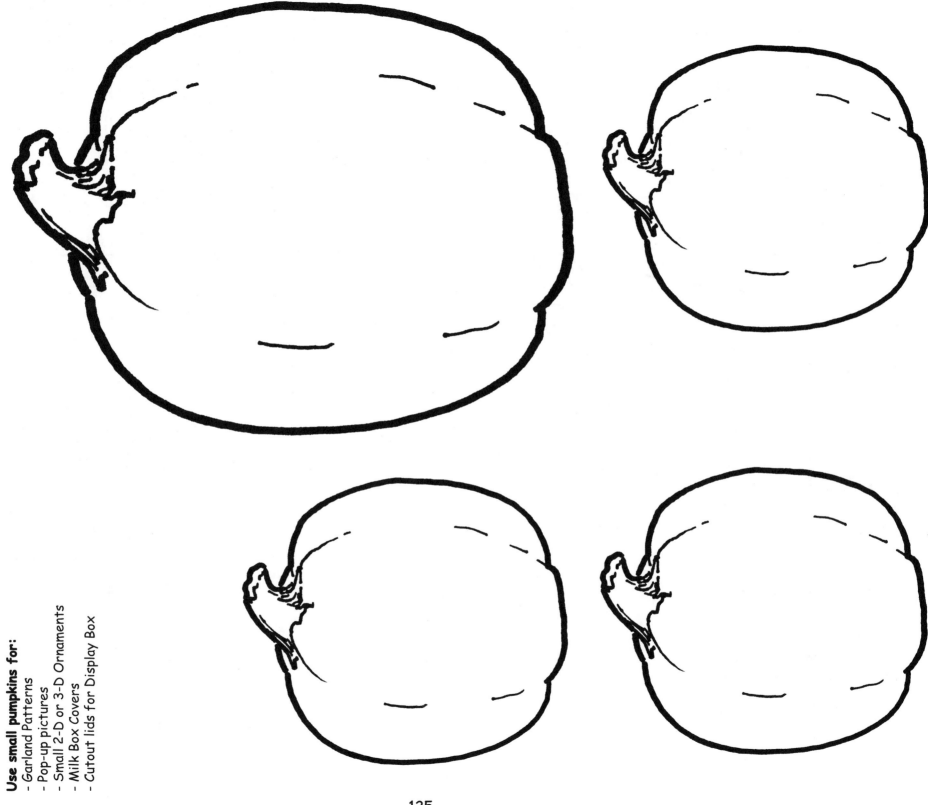

Use medium-sized pumpkins for:
- Picture Frame Books
- Large 2-D or 3-D ornaments

Use small pumpkins for:
- Garland Patterns
- Pop-up pictures
- Small 2-D or 3-D Ornaments
- Milk Box Covers
- Cutout lids for Display Box

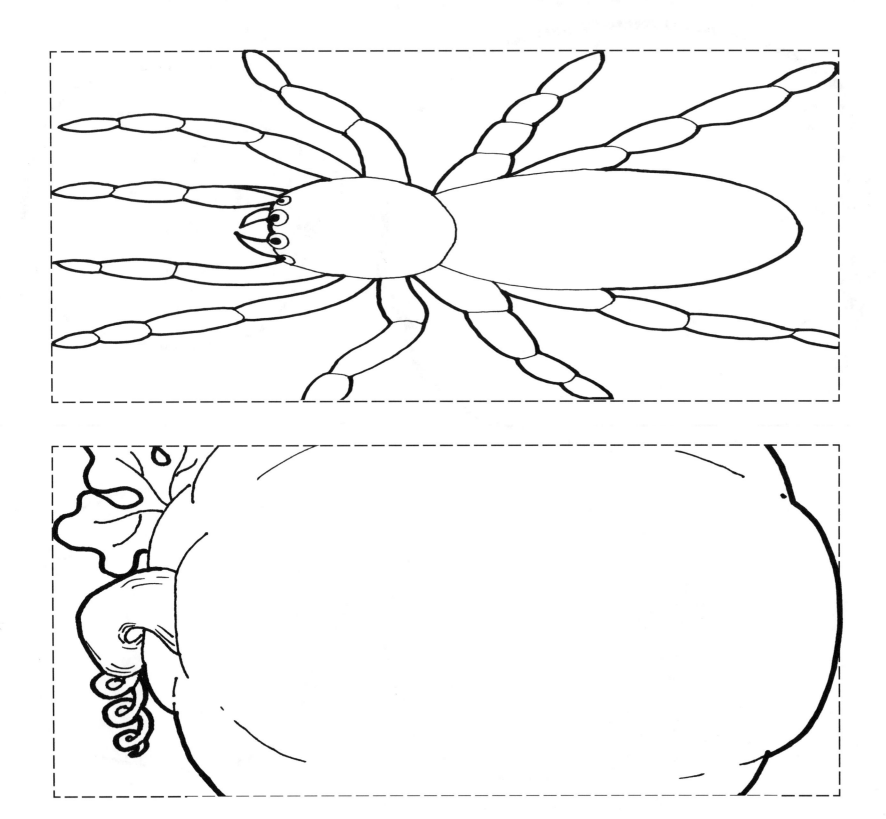

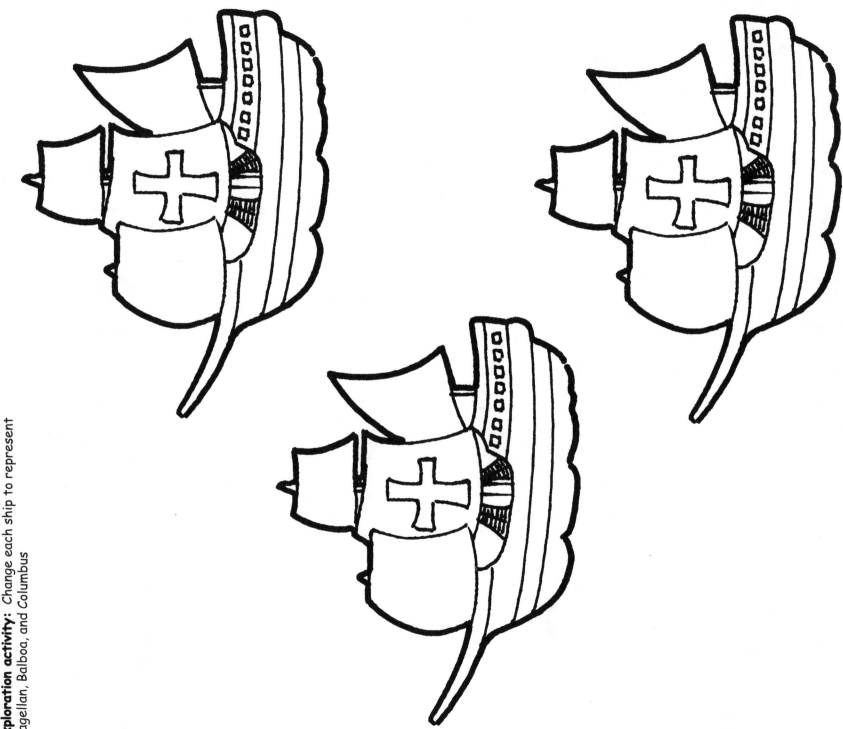

Use for:
-mobiles
-dioramas
-on a pyramid

Columbus Day activity: Niña, Pinta, and Santa Maria
Exploration activity: Change each ship to represent
Magellan, Balboa, and Columbus

November

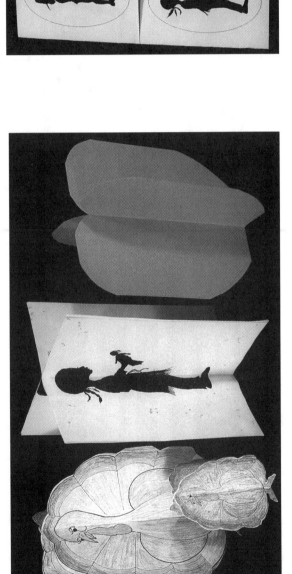

All Saint's Day = November 1

Day of the Dead = November 2 (Mexico)

Author's Day = November 2

Veteran's Day = November 11

Indian Heritage Day = November 25

Election Day = the Tuesday after the first Monday

National Children's Book Week (dates vary)

American Education Week = the week prior to Thanksgiving

National Stamp Collecting Week = begins the third Monday

Cat Week = begins the first Sunday

Thanksgiving = the fourth Thursday

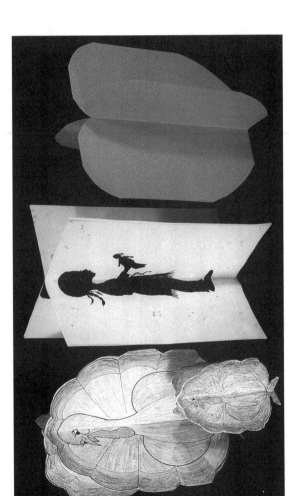

November Birthdays
Read, Research, Write

Important Note: It is nearly impossible to verify the actual date of birth of many historic figures. Different sources give differing dates for several birthdays in this list. Please note this during your class research. The birth years listed are more accurate than the birth months or days.

November 1, 1871: Stephen Crane, American author known for *The Red Badge of Courage*.
November 2, 1734: Daniel Boone, American frontiersman.
November 2, 1795: James Polk, 11th U. S. President.
November 2, 1840: Auguste Rodin, French sculptor.
November 2, 1865: Warren G. Harding, 29th U. S. President.
November 4, 1879: Will Rogers, American cowboy roper, 'cowboy philosopher', actor, and comedian.
November 6, 1854: John Philip Sousa, American band director and composer.
November 6, 1861: James Naismith, Canadian-American educator and inventor of basketball.
November 10, 1483: Martin Luther, German theologian and founder of Protestantism.
November 13, 1850: Robert Louis Stevenson, British author famous for his adventure stories.
November 14, 1765: Robert Fulton, American inventor, engineer, and painter.
November 14, 1840: Claude Monet, French impressionist painter.
November 15, 1887: Georgia O'Keeffe, American artist.
November 15, 1873: W.C. Handy, "Father of the Blues".
November 15, 1738: Sir William Herschel, British scientist, astronomer, organist and author.
November 19, 1831: James Garfield, 20th U. S. President
November 19, 1917: Indira Gandhi, daughter or Nehru, and leader of India.
November 23, 1804: Franklin Pierce, 14th U. S. President
November 24, 1784: Zachary Taylor, 12th U. S. President.
November 25, 1893: Robert Ripley, American creator of *Ripley's Believe It or Not*.
November 25, 1835: Andrew Carnegie, American industrialist and philanthropist.
November 29, 1832: Louisa May Alcott, American author.
November 29, 1898: C.S. Lewis, Irish-born author of the *Chronicles of Narnian*.
November 30, 1667: Jonathan Swift, Irish-born satirist and author of *Gulliver's Travels*.
November 30, 1835: Samuel Clemens (Mark Twain) American writer and humorist.
November 30, 1874: Winston Churchill, English statesman and WWII prime minister.

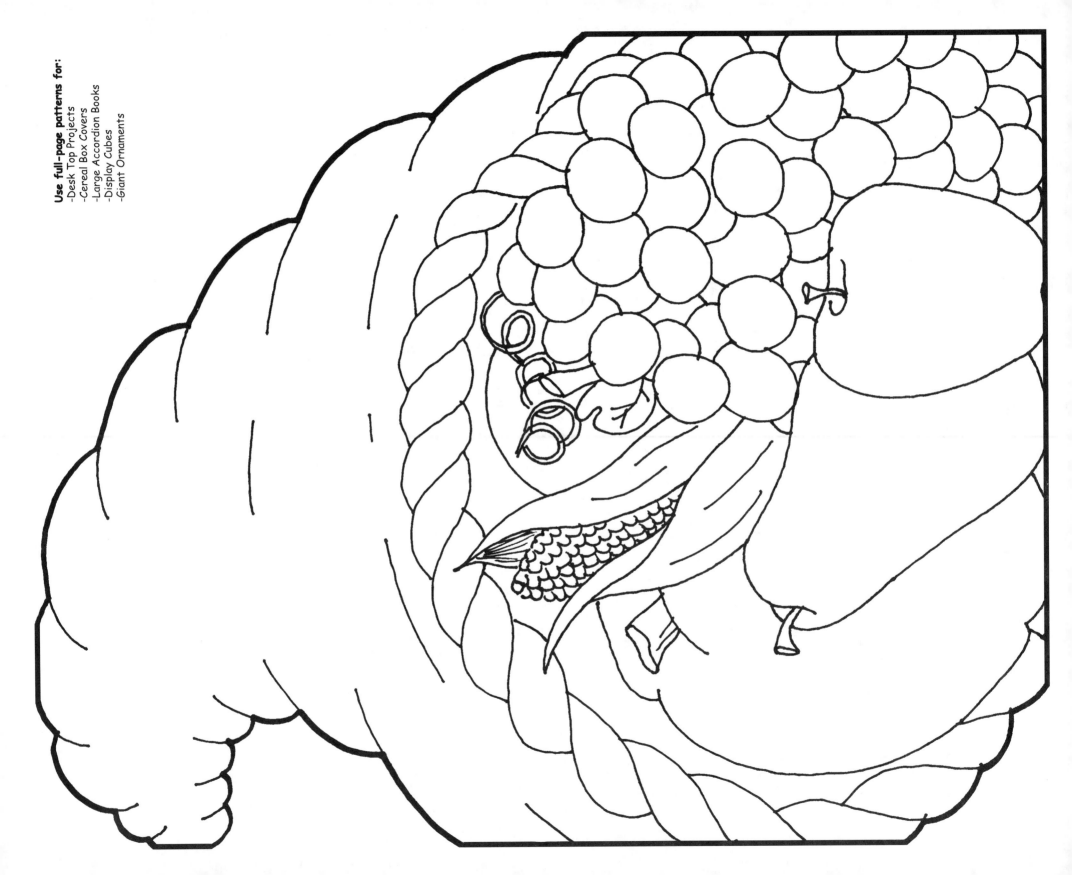

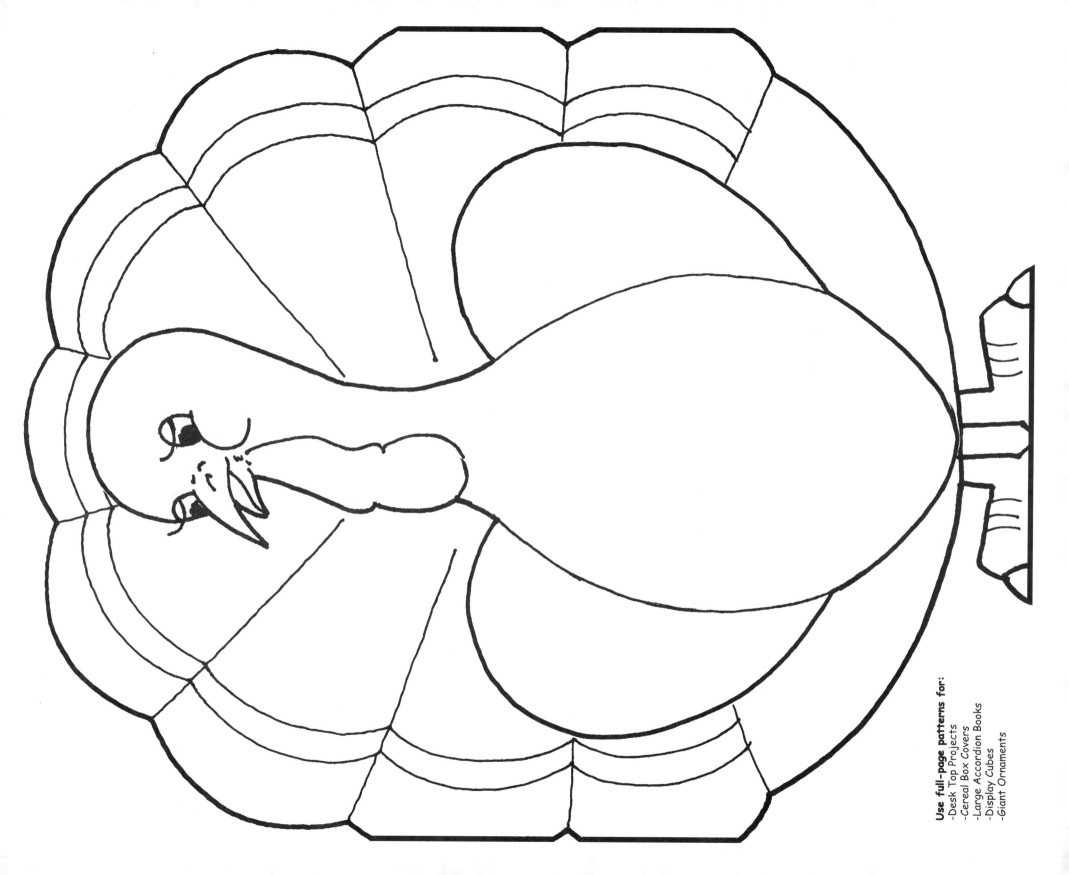

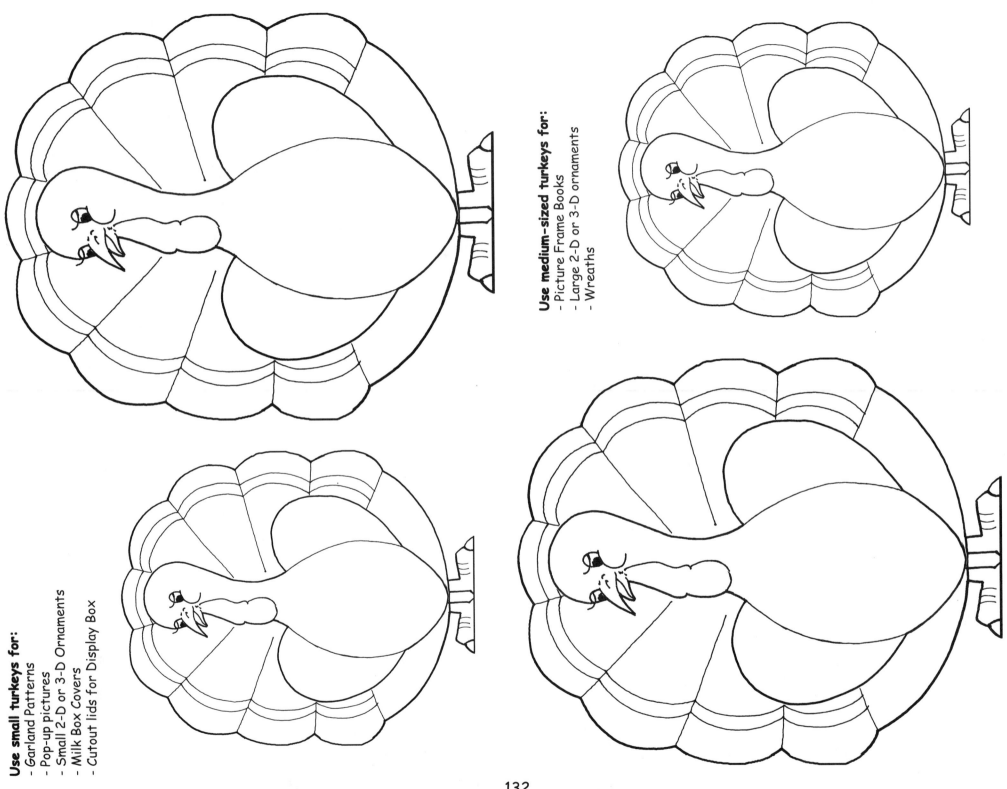

Use small turkeys for:
- Garland Patterns
- Pop-up pictures
- Small 2-D or 3-D Ornaments
- Milk Box Covers
- Cutout lids for Display Box

Use medium-sized turkeys for:
- Picture Frame Books
- Large 2-D or 3-D ornaments
- Wreaths

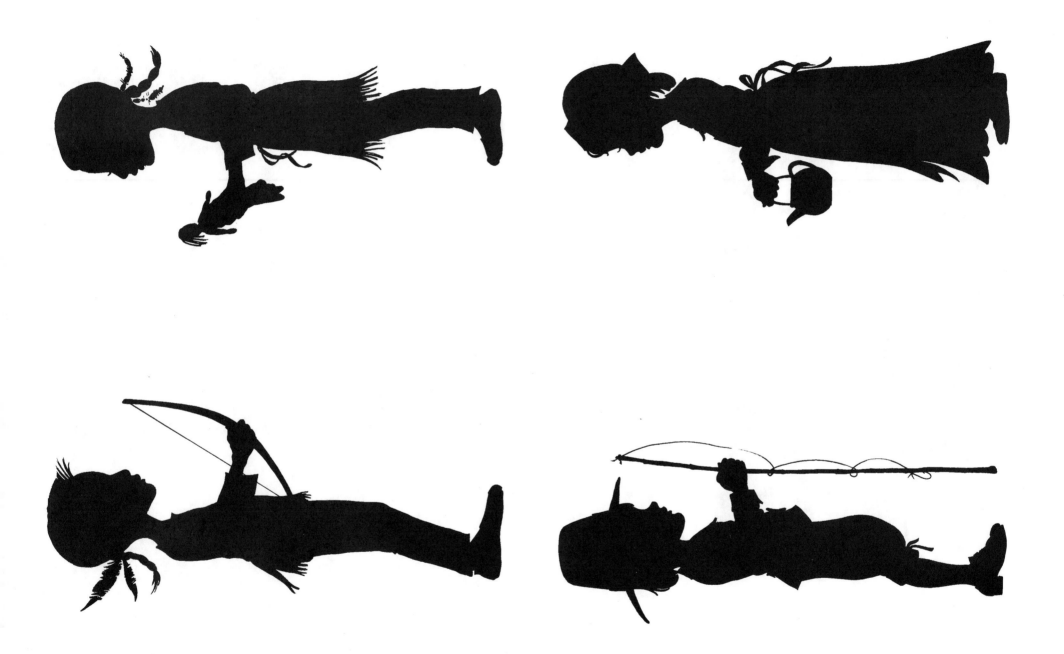

December

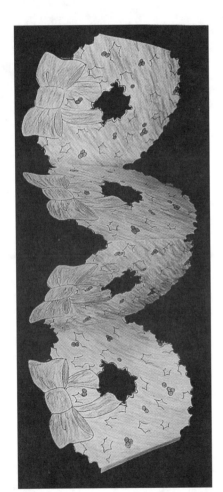

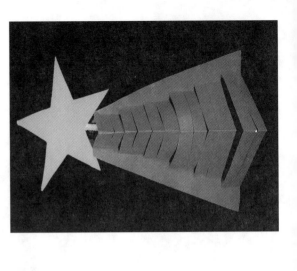

Human Rights Day = December 10

Feast of Our Lady of Guadalupe (Mexico) = December 12

Christmas Day = December 25

Hanukkah (Feast of Lights) = November or December

International Arbor Day = December 22

Kwanzaa = December 26 - January 1
(American Holiday observed around the world.)

New Year's Eve = December 31

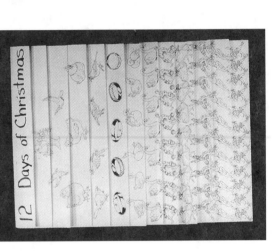

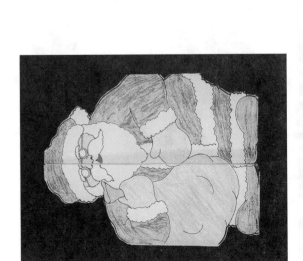

December Birthdays

Read, Research, Write

Important Note: It is nearly impossible to verify the actual date of birth of many historic figures. Different sources give differing dates for several birthdays in this list. Please note this during your class research. The birth years listed are more accurate than the birth months or days.

December 3, 1857: Joseph Conrad, Polish-born English author who wrote *Lord Jim*.

December 5, 1782: Martin Van Buren, 8th U. S. President.

December 6, 1886: Joyce Kilmer, American poet and journalist noted for the poem *Trees*.

December 8, 1765: Eli Whitney, American inventor of cotton gin.

December 8, 65 B. C.: Horace, Latin poet's approximate birthday.

December 9, 1848: Joel Chandler Harris, American journalist who recorded African American folktales.

December 9, 1608: John Milton, English poet and author of *Paradise Lost*.

December 10, 1830: Emily Dickinson, recluse American poet.

December 11, 1803: Hector Berlioz, French composer.

December 16, 1770: Ludwig von Beethoven, German composer.

December 16, 1775: Jane Austen, English author of *Pride and Prejudice* and *Emma*.

December 16, 1901: Margaret Mead, American social anthropologist.

December 17, 1807: John Greenleaf Whittier, American poet and reformer, called the Quaker Poet.

December 20, 1868: Harvey S. Firestone, American industrialist who developed rubber tires.

December 21, 1858: Giacomo Puccini, Italian operatic composer.

December 23, 1805: Joseph Smith, founder of the Mormon Church.

December 24, 1809: Kit Carson, American frontiersman, trapper, and guide.

December 25, 1642: Isaac Newton, English mathematician identified "law of gravity".

December 25, 1821: Clara Barton, founder of American Red Cross.

December 26, 1716: Thomas Gray, English poet. Wrote "Elegy Written in a Country Churchyard."

December 27, 1822: Louis Pasteur, French chemist and founder of the science of microbiology.

December 27, 1571: Johannes Kepler, German scientist, father of modern astronomy.

December 28, 1856: Woodrow Wilson, 28th U. S. President.

December 28, 1905: Earl "Fatha" Hines, American musician-composer.

December 29, 1808: Andrew Johnson, 17th U. S. President.

December 29, 1800: Charles Goodyear, American inventor of vulcanization process.

December 30, 1865: Rudyard Kipling, English author born in Bombay, India.

December 31, 1869: Henri Matisse, French painter and leader of Fauvism.

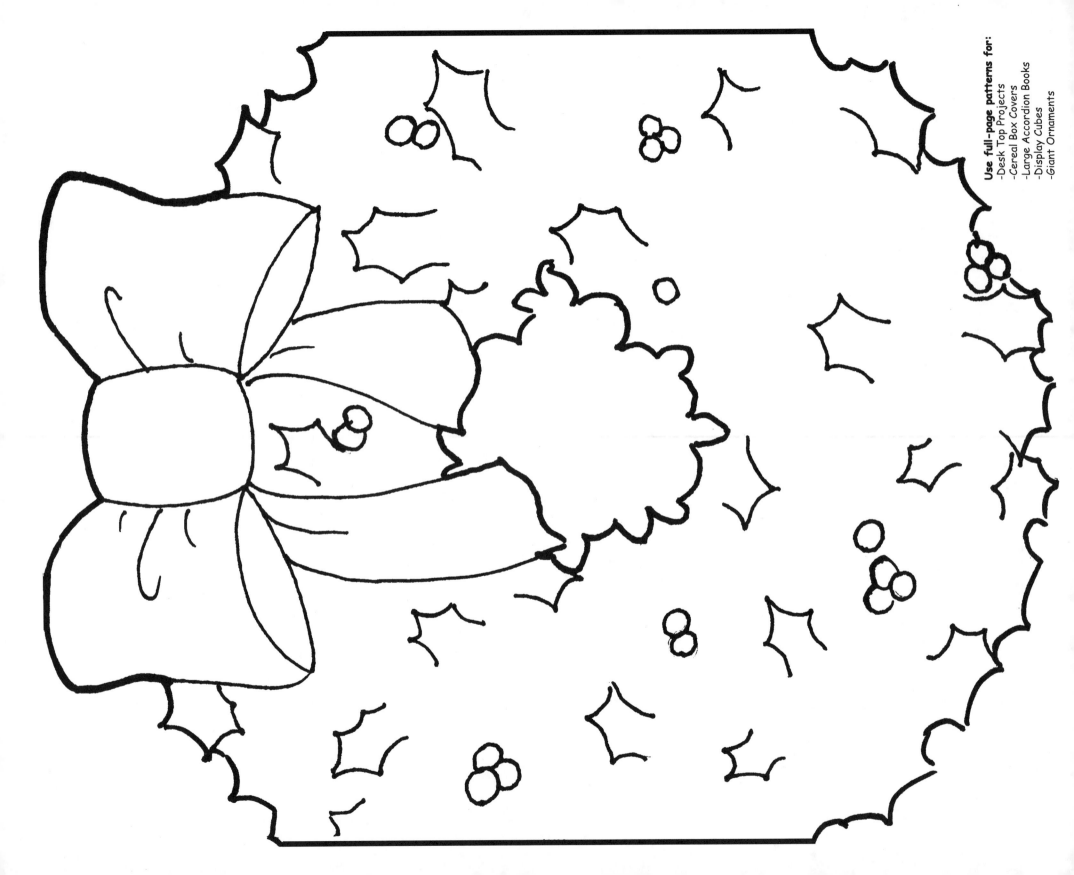

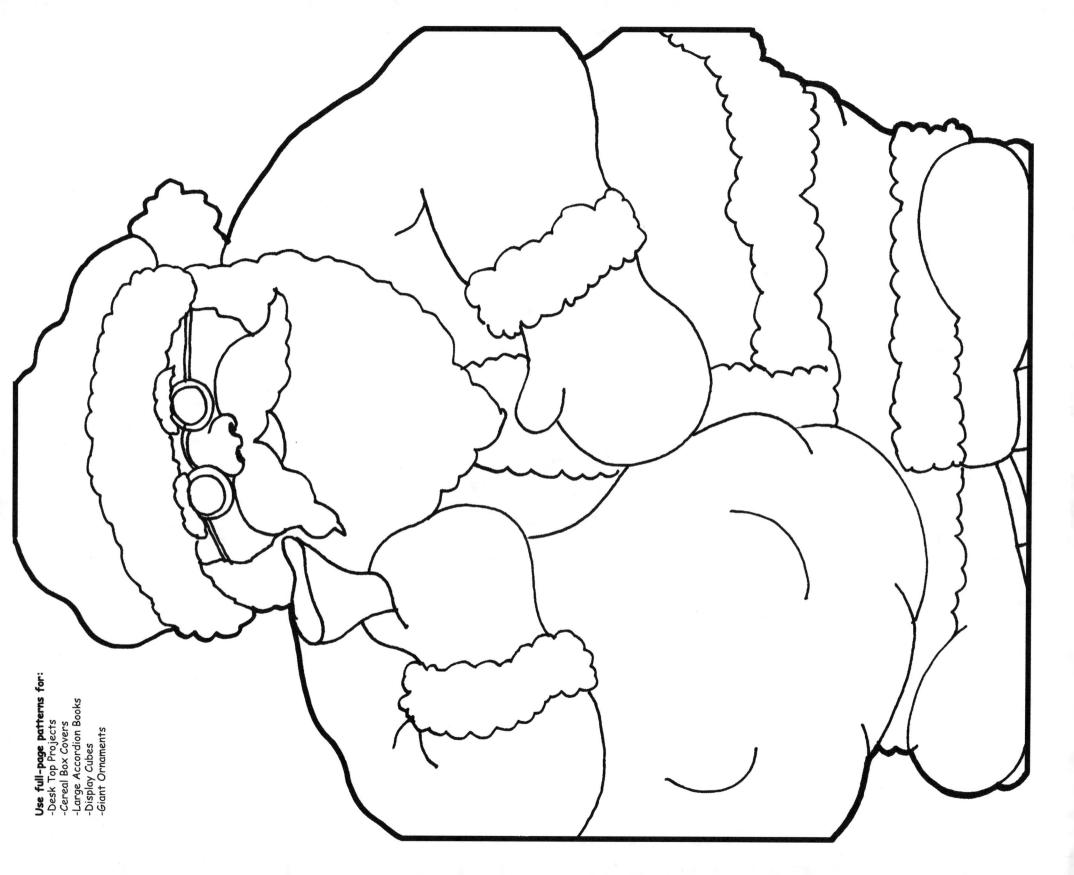

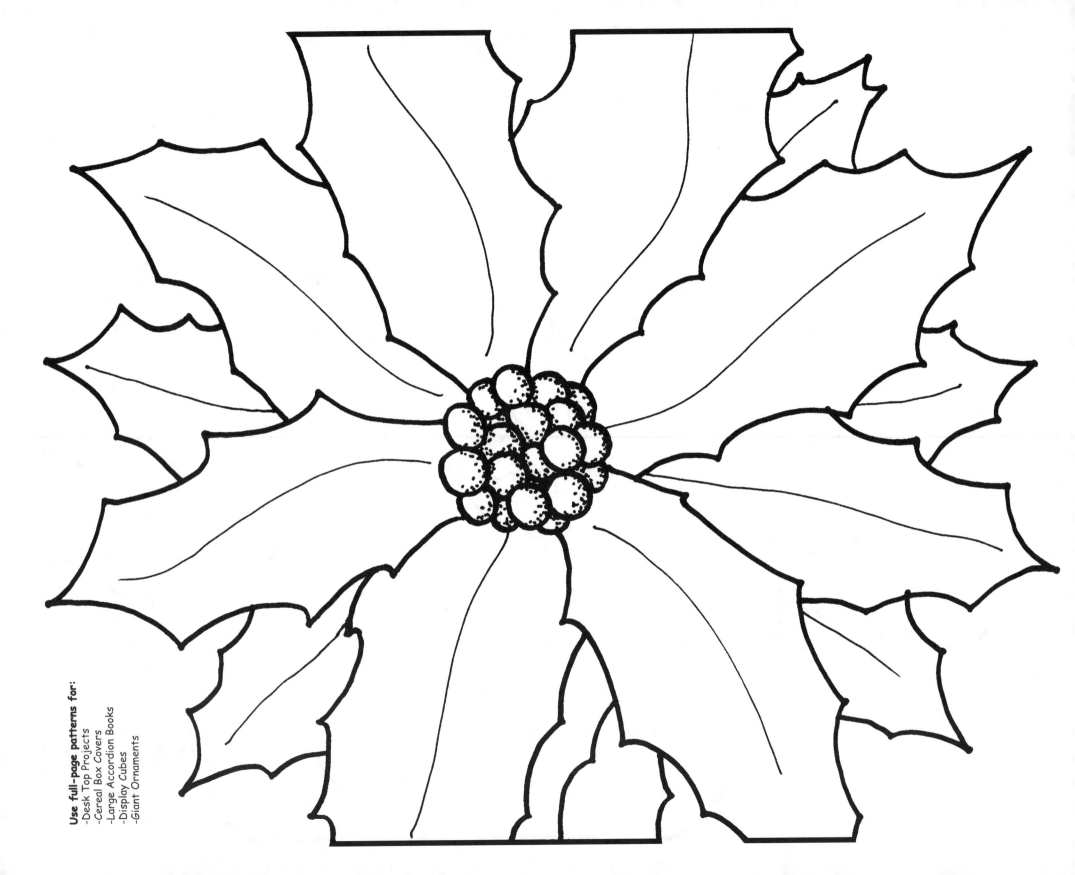

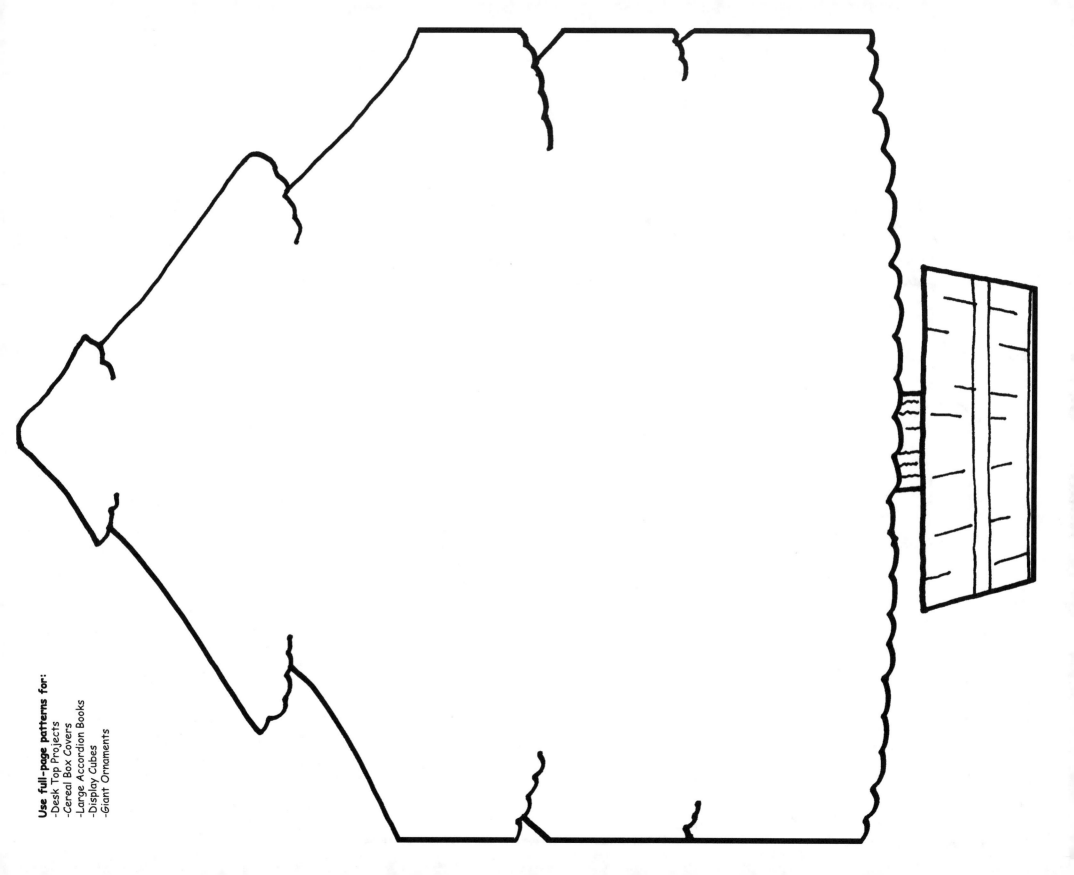

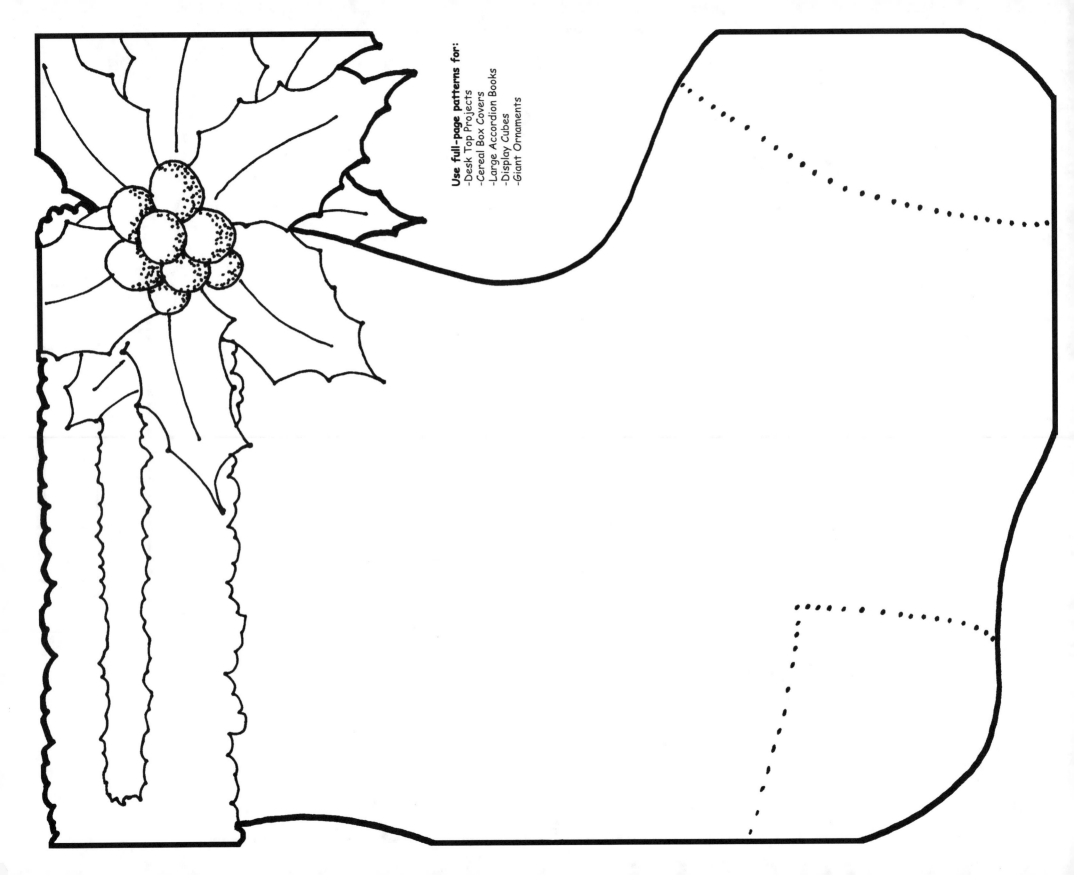

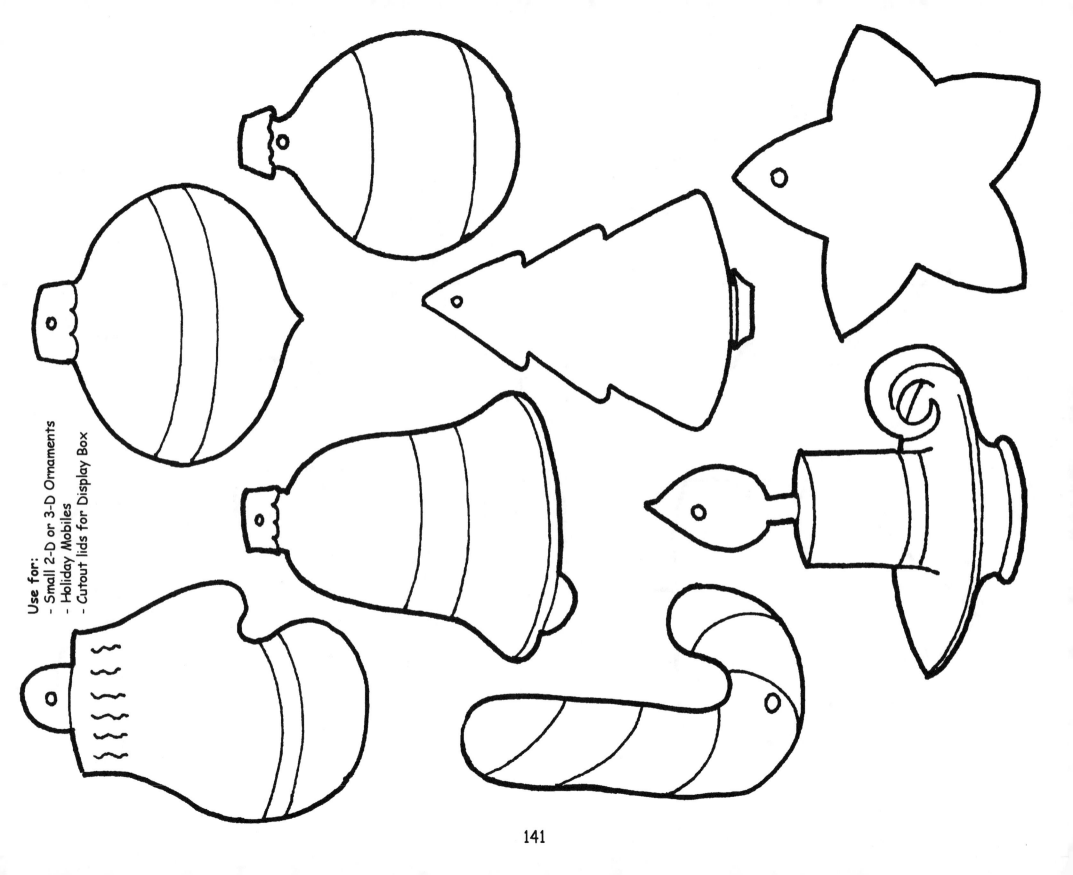

Use for:
- Small 2-D or 3-D Ornaments
- Holiday Mobiles
- Cutout lids for Display Box

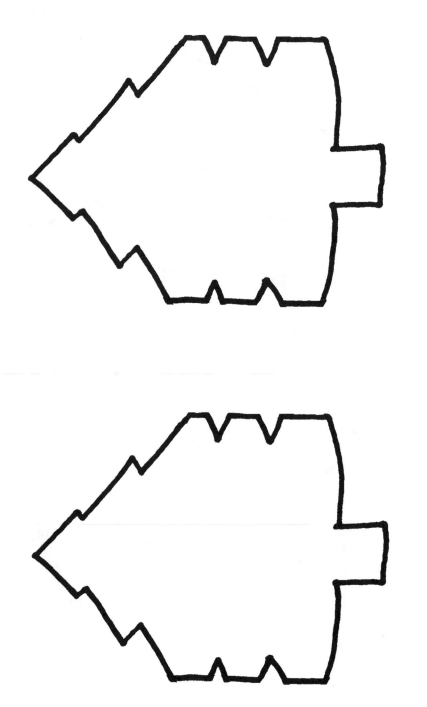

Use small gingerbread figures and trees for:
Garland Patterns
Pop-up pictures
Small 2-D or 3-D Ornaments
Milk Box Covers
Cutout lids for Display Box

Kwanzaa Candles

One for each of the Nguzo Saba, or Seven Principles:

 *umoja* = unity

 *kujichagulia* = self-determination

 *ujima* = collective work and responsibility

 *ujamaa* = cooperative economics

 *nia* = purpose

 *kuumba* = creativity

 *imani* = faith

Two Turtle Doves

Four Calling Birds

A Partridge In A Pear Tree

Three French Hens

144

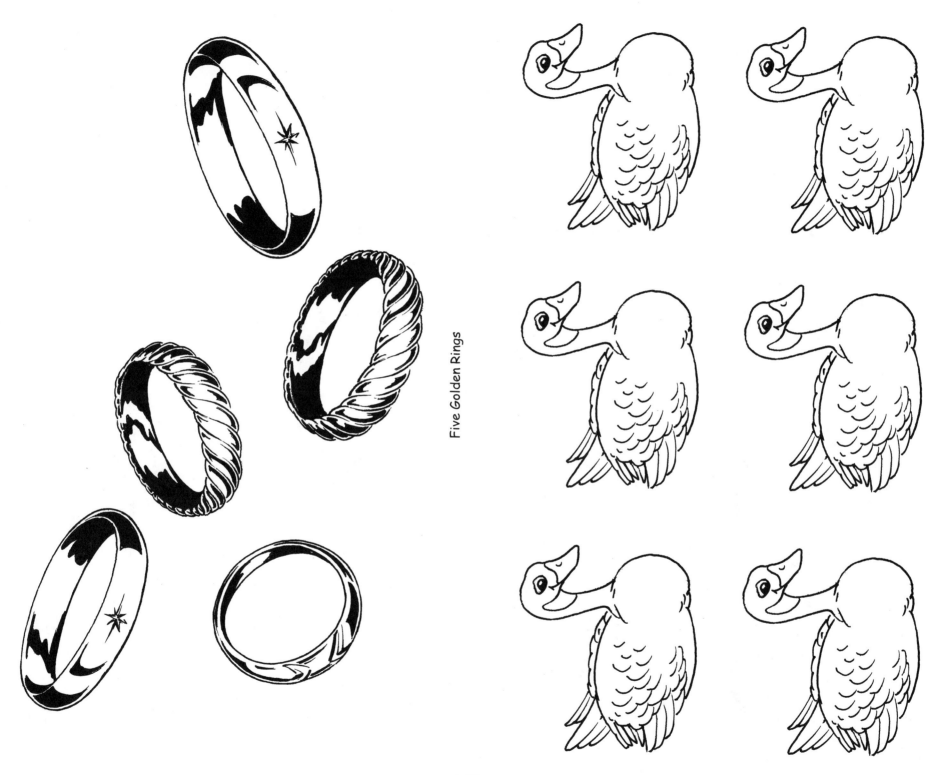

Five Golden Rings

Six Geese A Laying

145

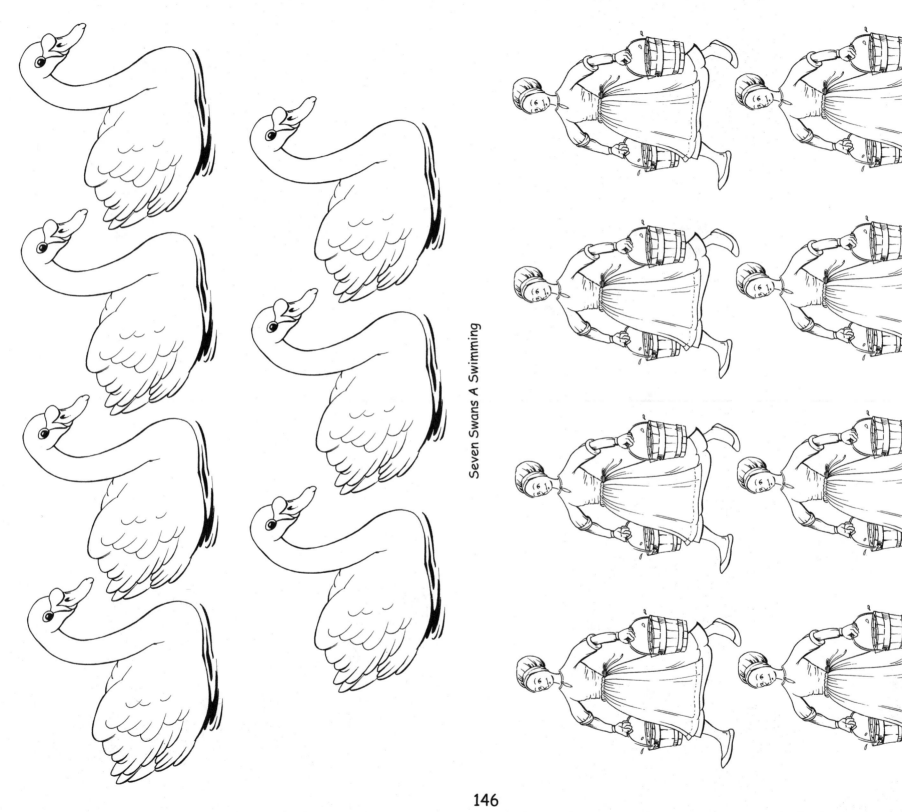

Seven Swans A Swimming

Eight Maids A Milking

The Twelve Days Of Christmas

Nine Ladies Dancing

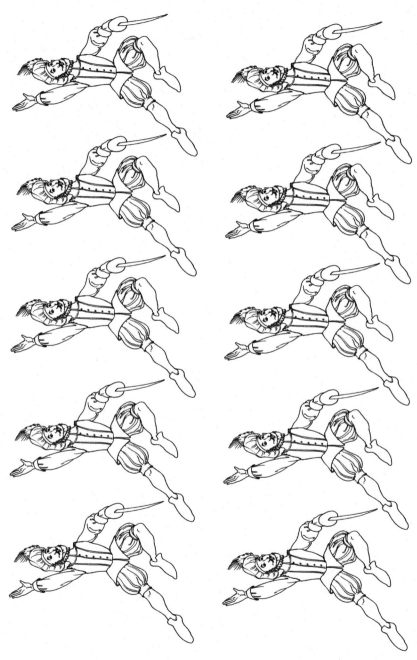

Ten Lords A Leaping

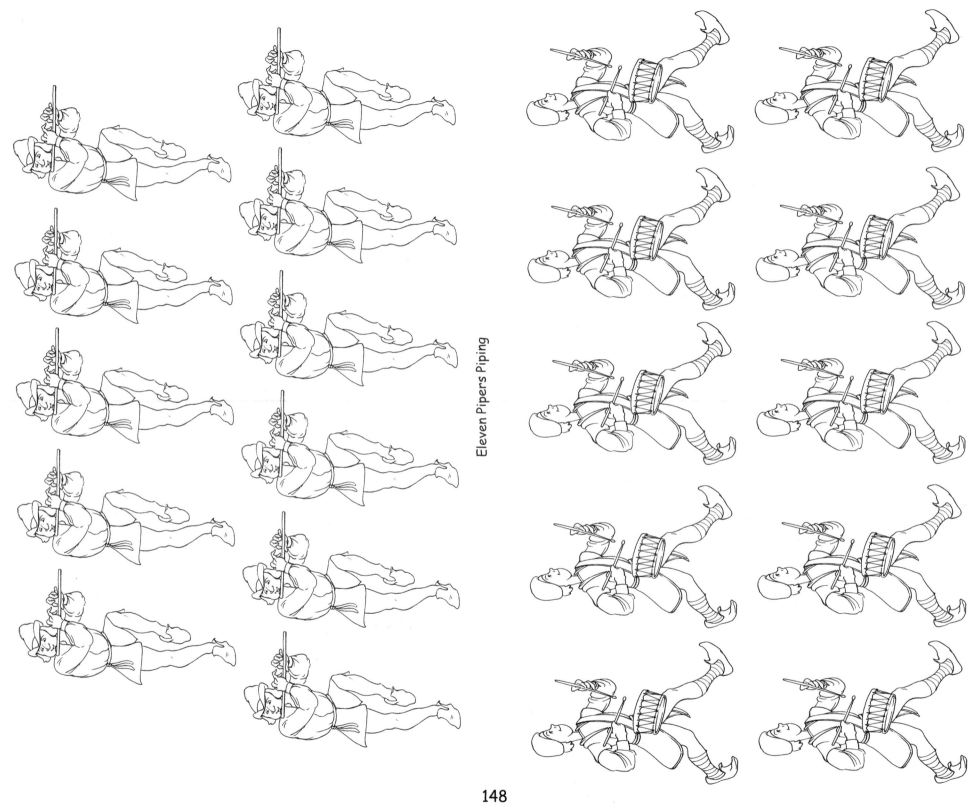

Eleven Pipers Piping

Twelve Drummers Drumming

148

Special Events

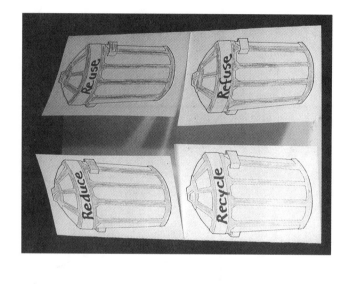

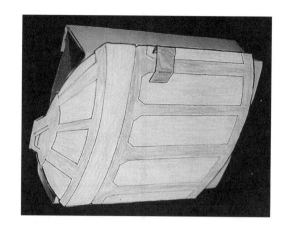

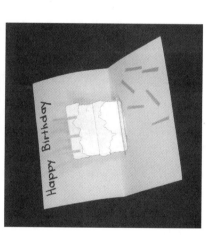

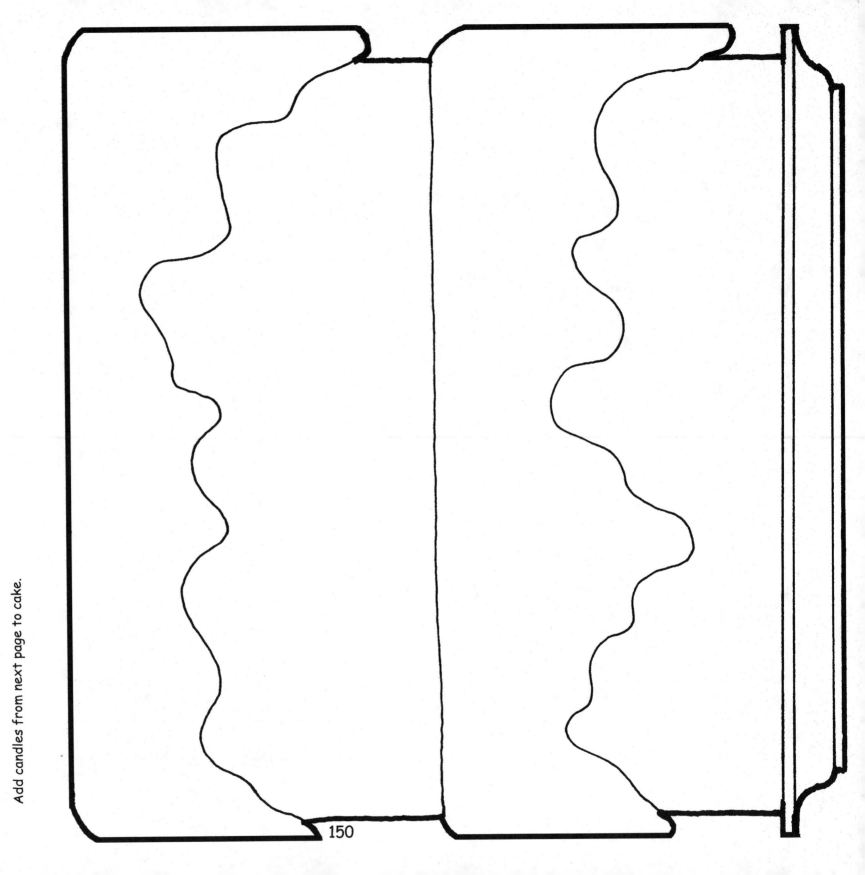

Add candles from next page to cake.

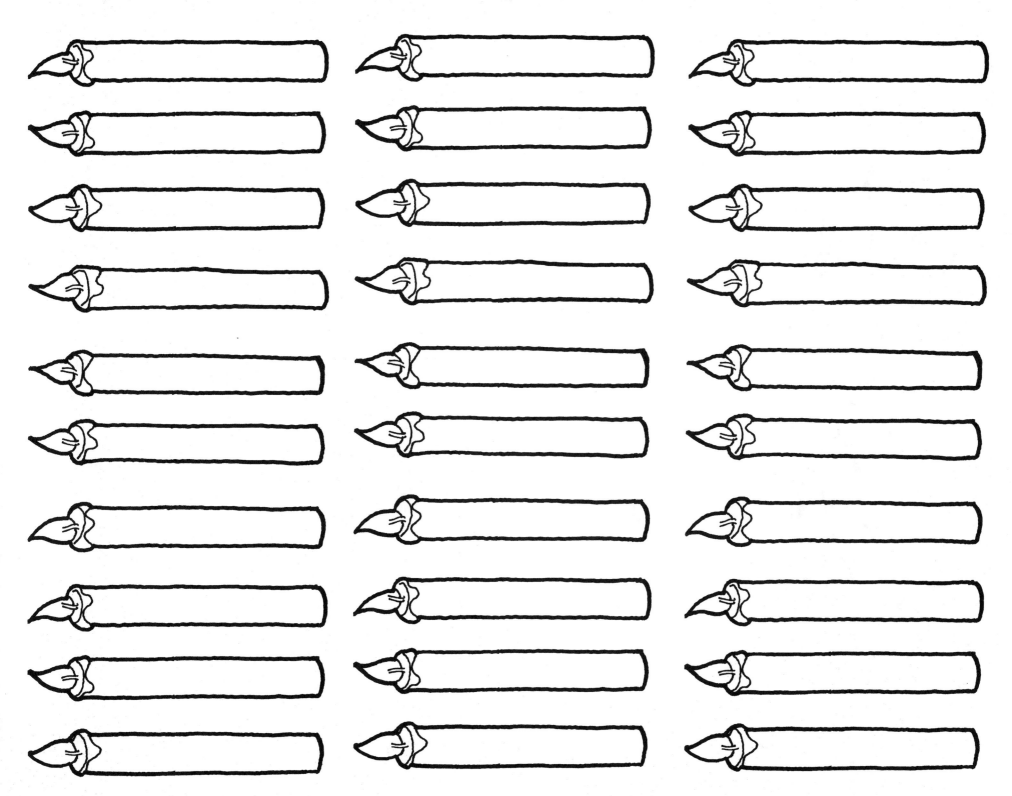

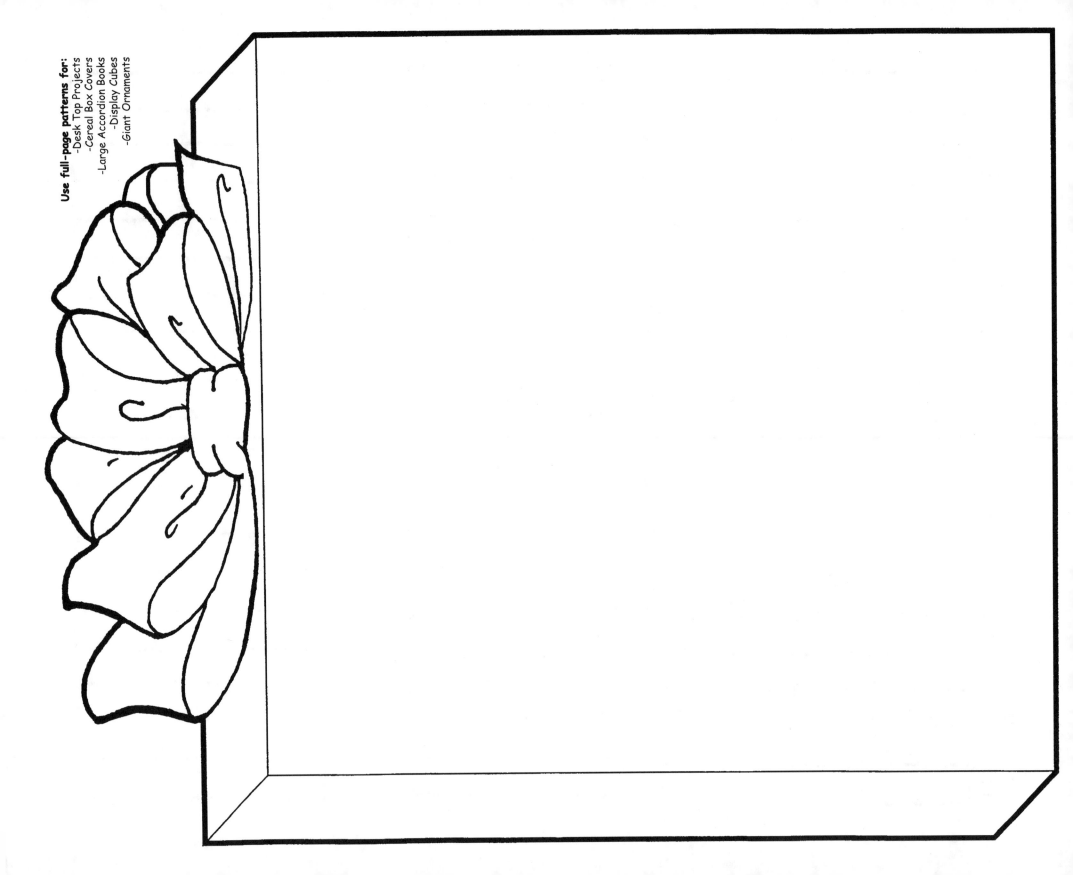

Use full-page patterns for:
-Desk Top Projects
-Cereal Box Covers
-Large Accordion Books
-Display Cubes
-Giant Ornaments

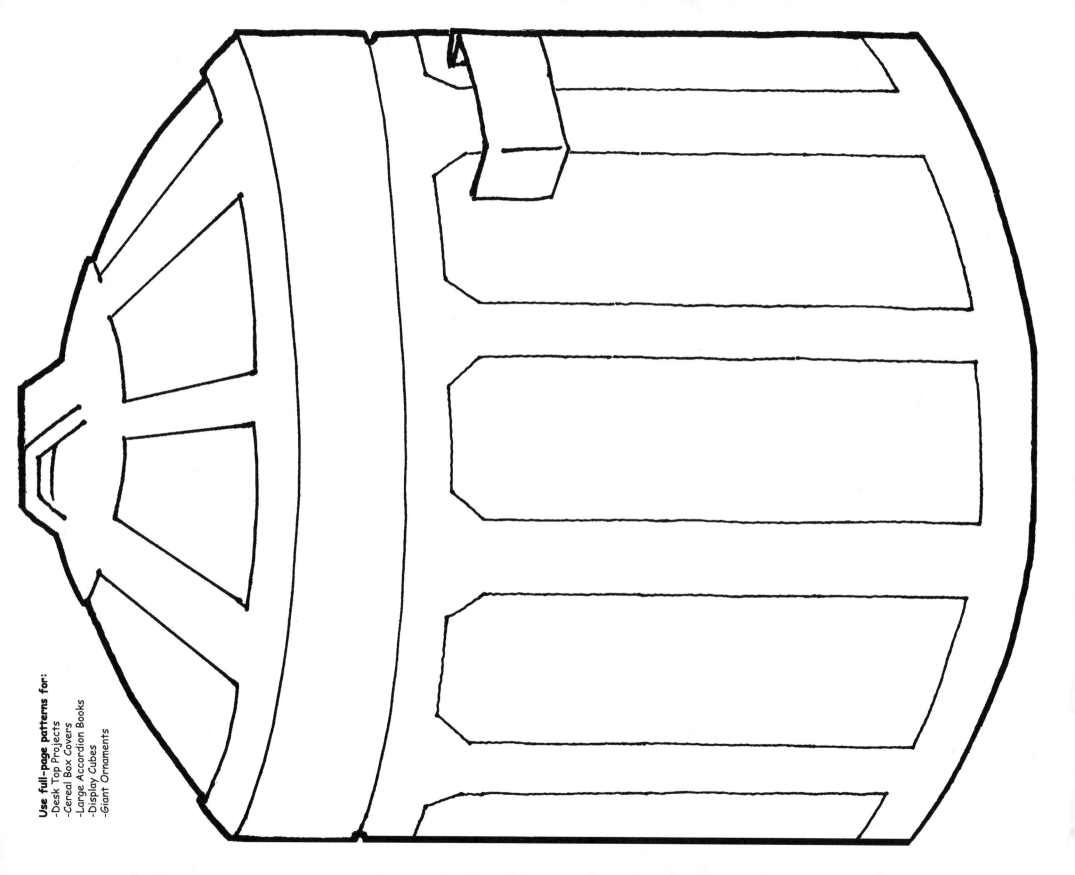

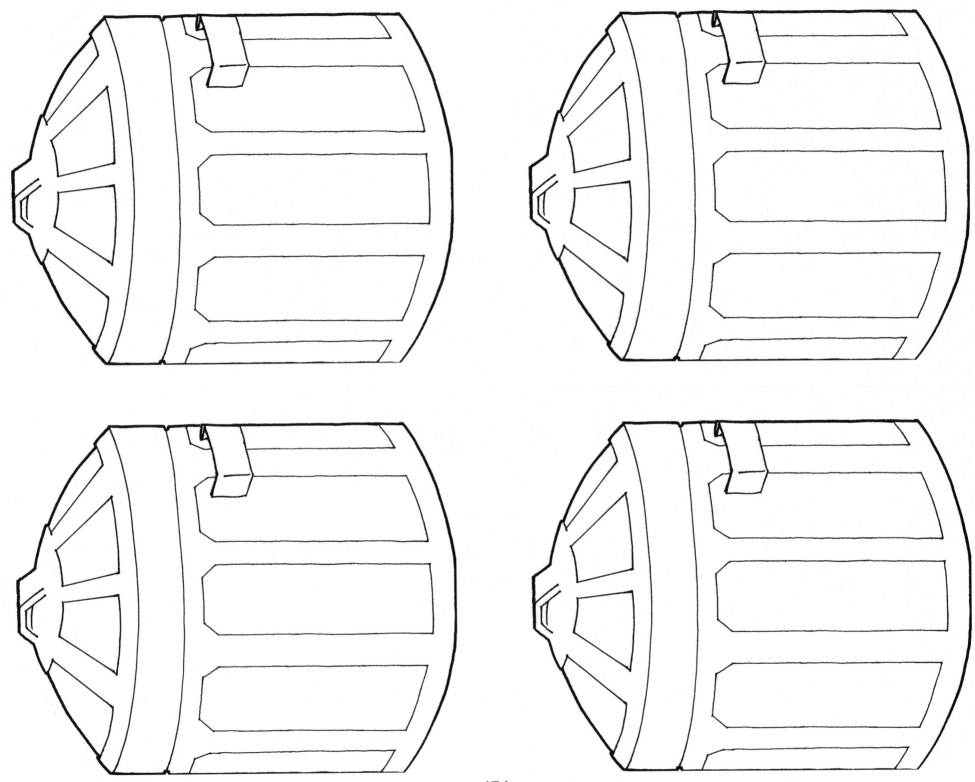

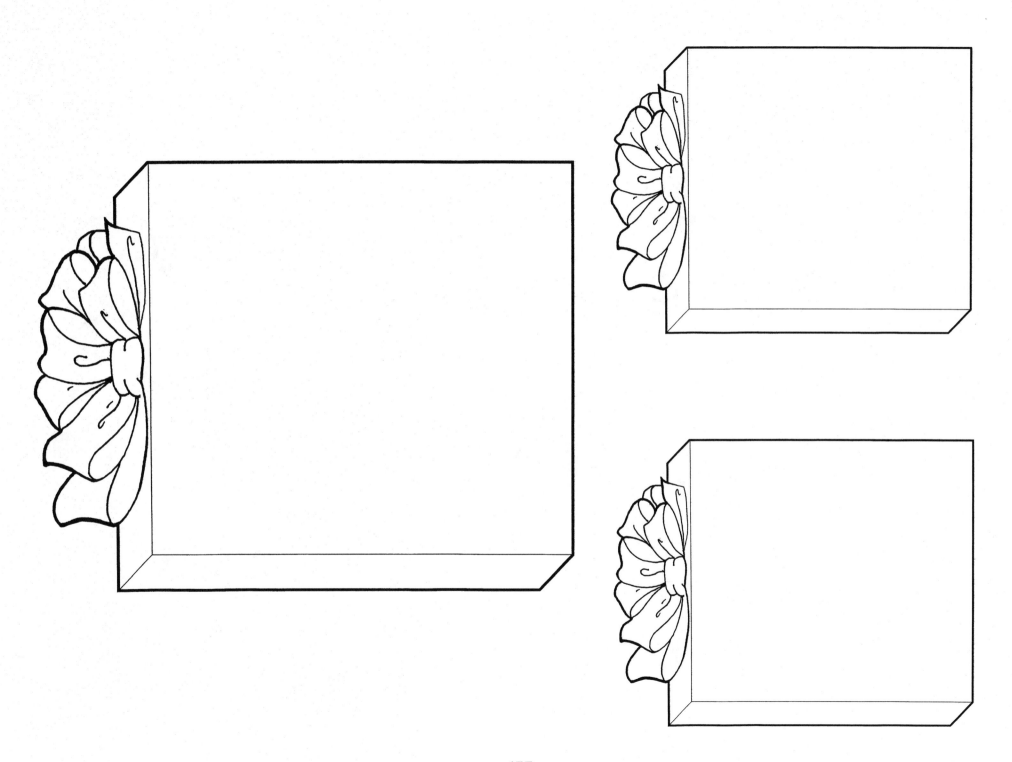

Religious Symbols

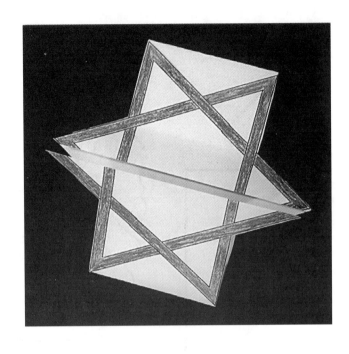

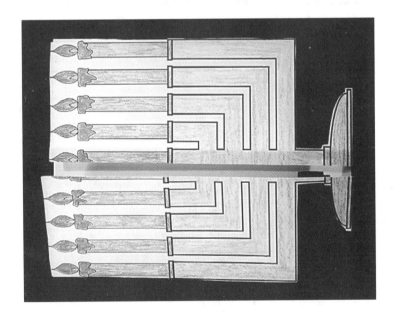

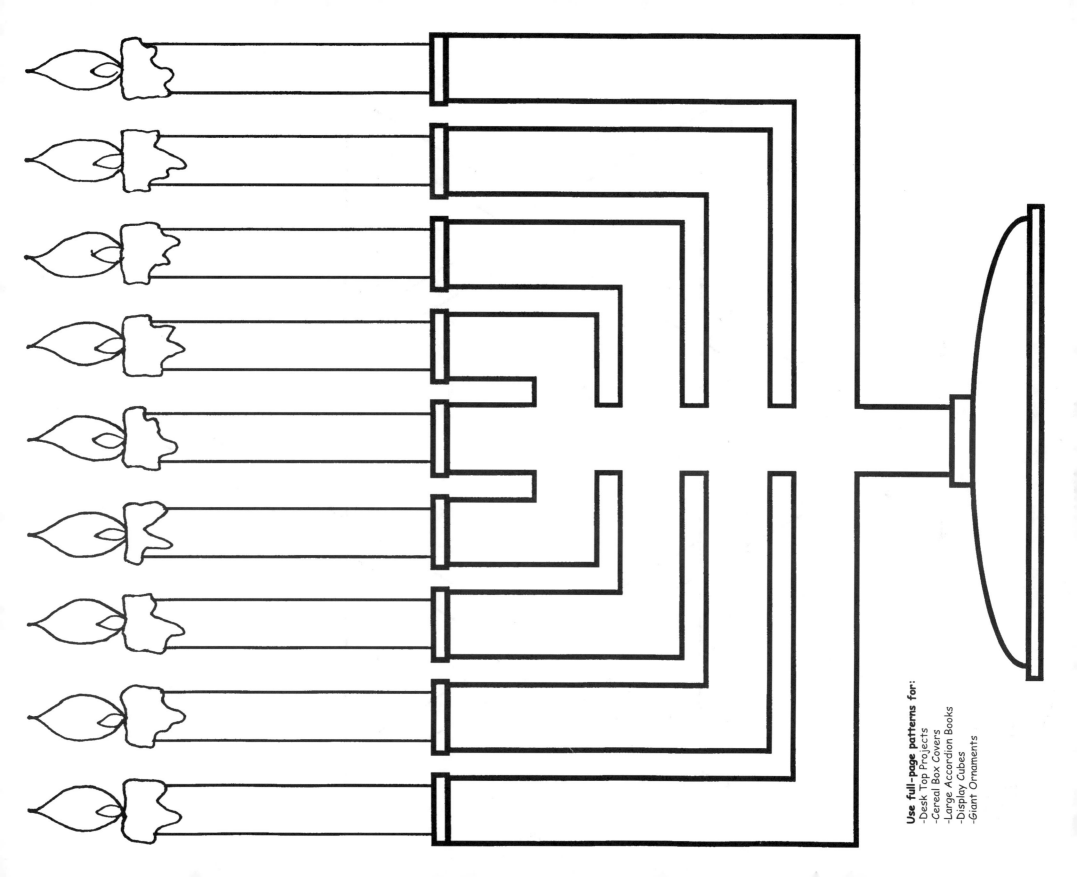

Use full-page patterns for:
-Desk Top Projects
-Cereal Box Covers
-Large Accordion Books
-Display Cubes
-Giant Ornaments

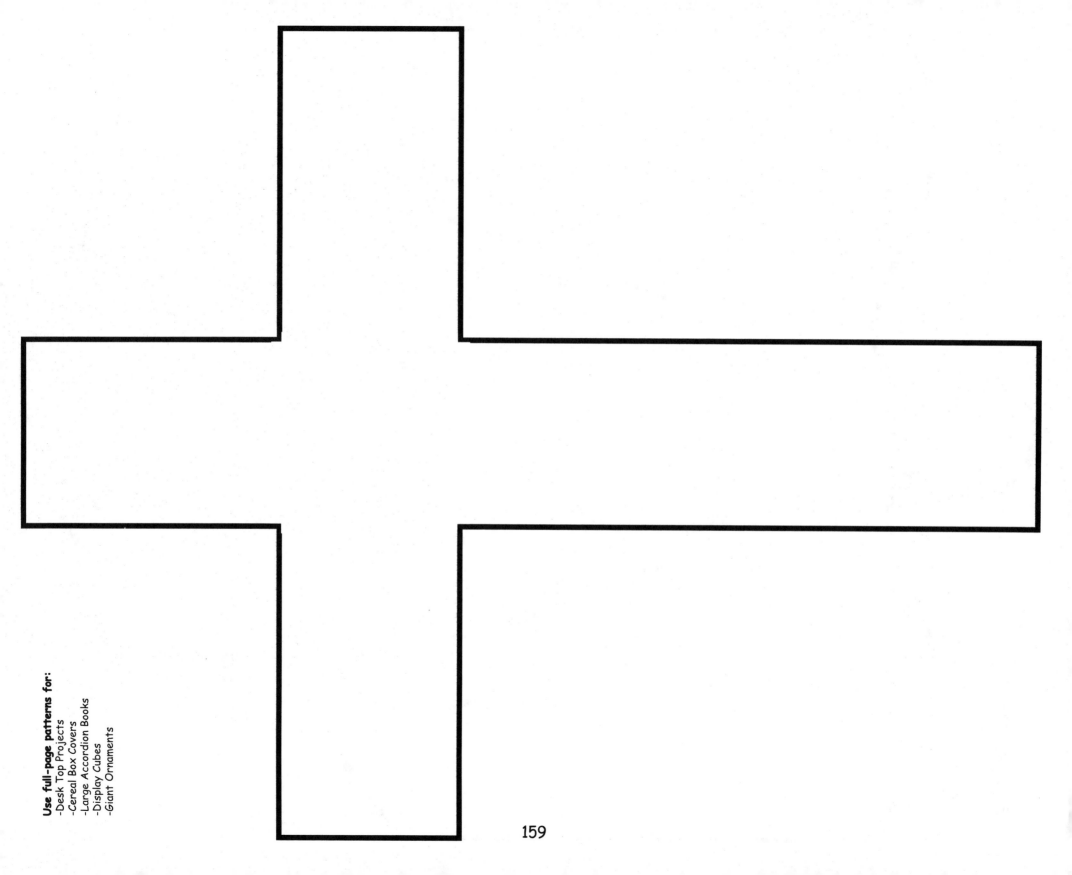

Use full-page patterns for:
-Desk Top Projects
-Cereal Box Covers
-Large Accordion Books
-Display Cubes
-Giant Ornaments

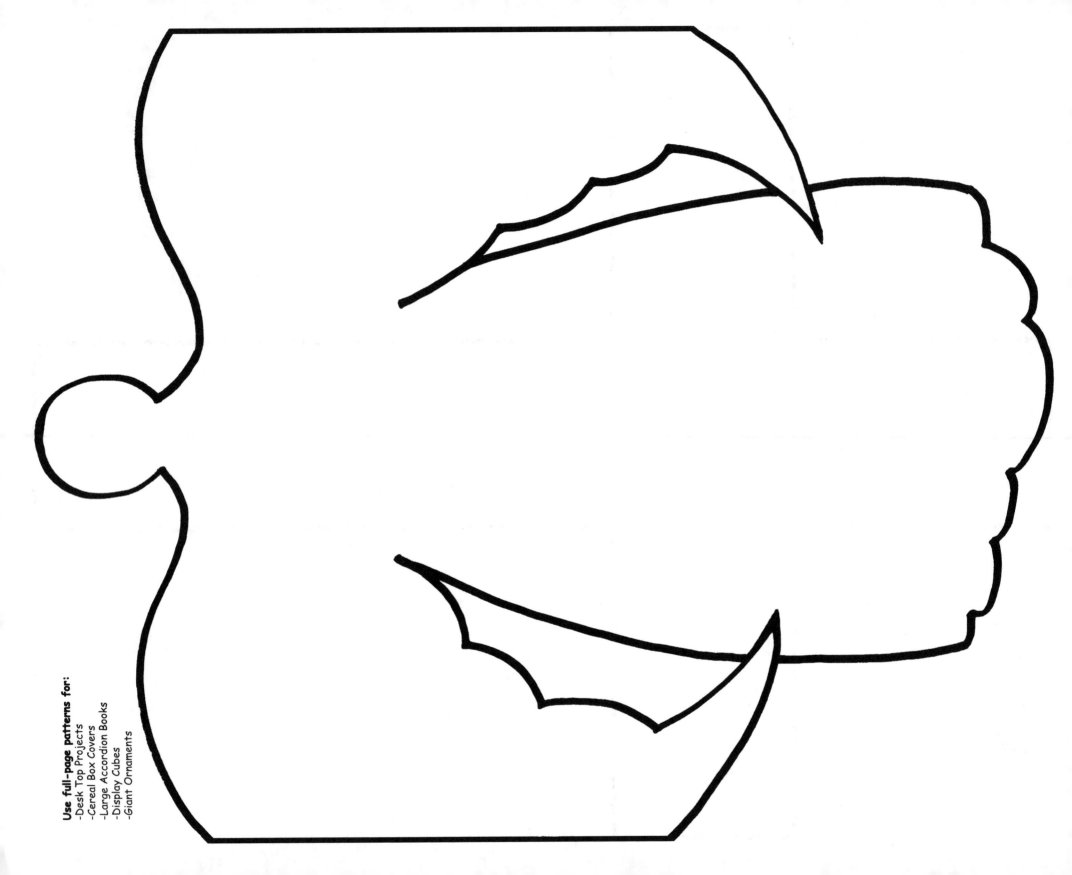

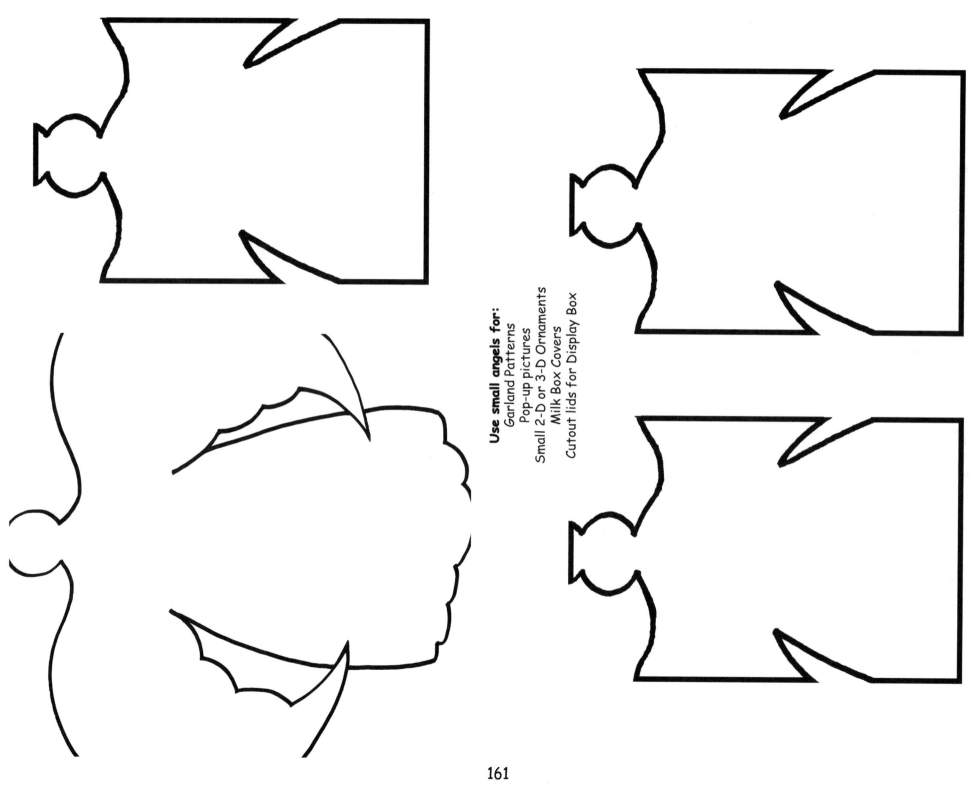

Use small angels for:
Garland Patterns
Pop-up pictures
Small 2-D or 3-D Ornaments
Milk Box Covers
Cutout lids for Display Box

Presidential Birthdays

Use For Creative Writing, Research Projects, & Timelines or Timetables

#	President	Birthday	Term
1:	George Washington	February 22, 1732	(Term: 1789-1797)
2:	John Adams	October 19, 1735	(Term: 1797-1801)
3:	Thomas Jefferso	April 13, 1743	(Term: 1801-1809)
4:	James Madison	March 16, 1751	(Term: 1809-1817)
5:	James Monroe	April 28, 1758	(Term: 1817-1825)
6:	John Quincy Adams	July 11, 1767	(Term: 1825-1829)
7:	Andrew Jackson	March 15, 1767	(Term: 1829-1837)
8:	Martin Van Buren	December 5, 1782	(Term: 1837-1841)
9:	William H. Harrison	February 9, 1773	(Term: Mar.-Apr.,1841)
10:	John Tyler	March 29, 1790	(Term: 1841-1845)
11:	James K. Polk	November 2, 1795	(Term: 1845-1849)
12:	Zachary Taylor	November 24, 1784	(Term: 1849-1850)
13:	Millard Fillmore	January 7, 1800	(Term: 1850-1853)
14:	Franklin Pierce	November 23, 1804	(Term: 1853-1857)
15:	James Buchanan	April 23, 1791	(Term: 1857-1861)
16:	Abraham Lincoln	February 12, 1809	(Term: 1861-1865)
17:	Andrew Johnson	December 29, 1808	(Term: 1865-1869)
18:	Ulysses S. Grant	April 27, 1822	(Term: 1869-1877)
19:	Rutherford B. Hayes	October 4, 1822	(Term: 1877-1881)
20:	James Garfield	November 19, 1831	(Term: Mar.-Sep. 1881)
21:	Chester A. Arthur	October 5, 1830	(Term: 1881-1885)
22:	Grover Cleveland	March 18, 1837	(Term: 1885-1889)
23:	Benjamin Harrison	August 20, 1833	(Term: 1889-1893)
24:	Grover Cleveland	March 18, 1837	(Term: 1893-1897)
25:	William McKinley	January 29, 1843	(Term: 1897-1901)
26:	Theodore Roosevelt	October 27, 1858	(Term: 1901-1909)
27:	William Howard Taft	September 15, 1857	(Term: 1909-1913)
28:	Woodrow Wilson	December 28, 1856	(Term: 1913-1921)
29:	Warren G. Harding	November 2, 1865	(Term: 1921-1923)
30:	Calvin Coolidge	July 4, 1872	(Term: 1923-1929)
31:	Herbert C. Hoover	August 10, 1874	(Term: 1929-1933)
32:	Franklin Delano Roosevelt	January 30, 1882	(Term: 1933-1945)
33:	Harry S. Truman	May 8, 1884	(Term: 1945-1953)
34:	Dwight D. Eisenhower	October 14, 1890	(Term: 1953-1961)
35:	John F. Kennedy	May 29, 1917	(Term: 1961-1963)
36:	Lyndon B. Johnson	August 27, 1908	(Term: 1963-1969)
37:	Richard M. Nixon	January 9, 1913	(Term: 1969-1974)
38:	Gerald R. Ford	July 14, 1913	(Term: 1974-1977)
39:	James Earl "Jimmy" Carter	October 1, 1924	(Term: 1977-1981)
40:	Ronald Reagan	February 6, 1911	(Term: 1981-1989)
41:	George Bush	June 12, 1924	(Term: 1989-1993)
42:	William Jefferson Clinton	August 19,1946	(Term: 1993-2001)

13 Colonies:
Ratification of the Constitution

Use For Research Projects, Timelines/Timetables, and Geography Integration

Listed In order of their ratification of the Constitution:

1	Delaware	December 7, 1787
2	Pennsylvania	December 12, 1787
3	New Jersey	December 18, 1787
4	Georgia	January 2, 1788
5	Connecticut	January 9, 1788
6	Massachusetts	February 6, 1788
7	Maryland	April 28, 1788
8	South Carolina	May 23, 1788
9	New Hampshire	June 21, 1788
10	Virginia	June 25, 1788
11	New York	July 26, 1788
12	North Carolina	November 21, 1789
13	Rhode Island	May 29, 1790

Dates For The Other 37 States

14	Vermont	March 4, 1791
15	Kentucky	June 1, 1792
16	Tennessee	June 1, 1796
17	Ohio	March 1, 1803
18	Louisiana	April 30, 1812
19	Indiana	December 11, 1816
20	Mississippi	December 10, 1817
21	Illinois	December 3, 1818
22	Alabama	December 14, 1819
23	Maine	March 15, 1820
24	Missouri	August 10, 1821
25	Arkansas	June 15, 1836
26	Michigan	January 26, 1837
27	Florida	March 3, 1845
28	Texas	December 29, 1845
29	Iowa	December 28, 1846
30	Wisconsin	May 29, 1848
31	California	September 9, 1850
32	Minnesota	May 11, 1858
33	Oregon	February 14, 1859
34	Kansas	January 29, 1861
35	West Virginia	June 19, 1863
36	Nevada	October 31, 1864
37	Nebraska	March 1, 1867
38	Colorado	August 1, 1876
39	North Dakota	November 2, 1889
40	South Dakota	November 2, 1889
41	Montana	November 9, 1889
42	Washington	November 11, 1889
43	Idaho	July 3, 1890
44	Wyoming	July 10, 1890
45	Utah	January 4, 1896
46	Oklahoma	November 16, 1907
47	New Mexico	January 5, 1912
48	Arizona	February 14, 1912
49	Alaska	January 3, 1959
50	Hawaii	August 21, 1959

International Holiday Dates

January

January 1: New Year's Day--North and South America, India, Indonesia, Japan, Korea, the Philippines, Singapore, Taiwan, and Thailand

January 1: Anniversary of the Revolution--Cuba

January 1: National Holiday--Haiti

January 1: Independence Day--Sudan

January 1: Independence Day--Western Samoa

January 2: Berchtoldstag--Switzerland

January 3: Genshi-Sai--Japan

January 4: Independence Day--Myanmar (formerly Burma)

January 5: Twelfth Night(Wassail Eve or Eve of Epiphany)--England

January 6: Epiphany, observed by Catholics--Europe and Latin America

January 15: Adults' Day--Japan

January 20: St. Agnes Eve--Great Britain

January 26: Republic Day--India

January 31: Independence Day--Nauru or Naoero (Pacific Island)

January: Australia Day (Last Monday of the month)

Jan-Feb: Chinese New Year and Vietnamese New Year (Tet)

International Holiday Dates

February

February:	Hamstrom (first Monday)--Switzerland
February 3:	Setsubun (Bean-throwing Festival)--Japan
February 4:	National Holiday--Sri Lanka
February 5:	Promulgation of the Constitution--Mexico
February 5:	Anniversary of the Liberation of the Republic--San Marino
February 6:	Waitangi Day or New Zealand Day
February 7:	Independence Day--Grenada
February 11:	National Foundation Day--Japan
February 11:	Victory of the Islamic Revolution--Iran
February 18:	Independence Day--Gambia
February 16:	National Holiday--Lithuania
February 22:	Independence Day--St. Lucia
February 23:	National Day--Brunel
February 23:	Republic Day--Guyana
February 24:	National Holiday--Estonia
February 25:	National Day--Kuwait
February 27:	Independence Day--Dominican Republic

International Holiday Dates

March

March 1:	Independence Movement Day--Korea
March 1:	Constitution Day--Panama
March 2:	Declaration of People's Power--Libya
March 3:	National Holiday--Bulgaria
March 3:	National Holiday--Morocco
March 6:	National Day--Ghana
March 8:	International Women's Day--all U.N. member nations
March 12:	Independence Day--Mauritius
March 12:	Renovation Day--Gabon
March 17:	St. Patrick's Day--Ireland
March 19:	St. Joseph's Day--Colombia, Costa Rica, Italy, and Spain
March 21:	Benito Juarez's Birthday--Mexico
March 21:	National Holiday--Namibia
March 22:	Arab League Day--Arab League countries
March 23:	Pakistan Day
March 25:	Independence Day--Greece
March 25:	Lady Day (Quarter Day)--Great Britain
March 26:	Fiesta del Arbol (Arbor Day)--Spain
March 26:	National Day--Bangladesh
March 28:	British EvacuationDay--Libya
March 29:	Youth and Martyrs' Day--Taiwan
March 30:	Muslim New Year--Indonesia
March 31:	Freedom Day--Malta
March or April:	Carnival/Lent/Easter--Christian countries.

167

International Holiday Dates

April

April 1: Victory Day--Spain
April 1: April Fool's Day--United States and Great Britain
April 1: Islamic Republic Day--Iran
April 4: Independence Day--Senegal
April 4: Liberation Day--Hungary
April 5: Arbor Day--Korea
April 6: Van Riebeeck Day--South Africa
April 7: World Health Day--all U.N. member nations
April 8: Buddha's Birthday--Korea and Japan
April 8: Hana Matsuri (Flower Festival)--Japan
April 14: Pan American Day--North and South America
April 16: Birthday of the Queen--Denmark
April 17: National Holiday--Cambodia
April 17: Independence Day--Syria
April 18: National Holiday--Zimbabwe
April 19: Declaration of Independence Day--Venezuela
April 19: Republic Day--Sierra Leone
April 22: Queen Isabella Day--Spain
April 23: St. George's Day--England
April 25: Liberation Day--Italy
April 25: ANZAC Day--Australia and New Zealand
April 25: National Holiday--Portugal
April 26: Union Day--Tanzania
April 27: National Holiday--Afghanistan
April 27: Independence Day--Togo
April 29: Emperor's Birthday--Japan
April 30: Queen's Day--Netherlands
April 30: Walpurgis Night--Germany and Scandinavia
April 30: King's Birthday--Sweden

International Holiday Dates

May

May:	Constitution Day (first Monday)--Japan
May 1:	May Day-Labor Day--most of Europe and Latin America, Commonwealth of Independent States
May 1:	National Holiday--Marshall Islands
May 3:	National Holiday--Poland
May 5:	Children's Day--Japan and Korea
May 5:	Victory of General Zaragosa Day--Mexico
May 5:	Liberation Day--The Netherlands
May 8:	V-E Day--Europe
May 9:	Victory over Fascism Day--Commonwealth of Independent States
May 9:	Liberation Day--Czechoslovakia
May 10:	National Holiday--Micronesia
May 14,15:	Independence Days--Paraguay
May 14:	Israel declared independence (1948)
May 17:	Constitution Day--Norway
May 17:	Constitution Day--Nauru or Naoero (Pacific Island)
May 20:	National Day--Cameroon
May 22:	Independence Day--Sri Lanka
May 25:	Independence Day--Argentina
May 25:	Independence Day--Jordan
May 31:	Republic Day--South Africa

International Holiday Dates

June

June 1: Independence Day--Tunisia
June 1: National Holiday--Western Somoa
June 2: Republic Day--Italy
June 5: Constitution Day--Denmark
June 5: World Environment Day--U.N. member nations
June 5: Constitution Day--Seychelles
June 6: Memorial Day--Korea
June 6: Sweden Day or Flag Day--Sweden
June 7: National Holiday--Chad
June 8: Muhammad's Birthday--Indonesia
June 10: Portugal Day
June 12: Republic Day--Commonwealth of Independent States
June 12: Independence Day--Philippines
June 16: Soweto Day--U. N. member nations
June 16: U.S. Evacuation Day--Libya
June 16: Birthday of the Queen--United Kingdom
June 17: Anniversary of the Establishment of the Republic--Iceland
June 20: Flag Day--Argentina
June 23: Grand Duke's birthday--Luxembourg
June 24: National Holiday--Spain
June 25: Independence Day--Mozambique
June 26: Independence Day--Madagascar
June 27: National Holiday--Djibouti
June 29: Feast of Saints Peter and Paul--Chile, Colombia, Costa Rica, Italy, Peru, Spain, Vatican City, and Venezuela
June 29: Independence Day--Seychelles
June 30: Independence Day--Zaire
Mid-June: Midsummer Celebrations--Sweden

International Holiday Dates

July

July 1: Half-year Holiday--Hong Kong
July 1: Bank Holiday--Taiwan
July 1: Dominion Day or Canada Day--Canada
July 1: Independence Day--Burundi
July 1: National Day--Rwanda
July 4: King's Birthday--Tonga
July 5: Independence Day--Venezuela
July 5: Independence Day--Cape Verde Islands
July 6: National Holiday--Comoros
July 6: Republic Day--Malawi
July 7: Independence Day--Solomon Islands
July 9: Independence Day--Argentina
July 10: Bon (Feast of Fortune)--Japan
July 10: Independence Day--Bahamas
July 11: People's Revolution Day--Mongolia
July 12: Orangemen's Day--Northern Ireland
July 12: Independence Day--Sao Tome and Principe
July 14: Bastille Day or National Day--France
July 17: Constitution Day--Korea
July 14 & 17: National Holidays to commemorate revolutions--Iraq
July 18: National Day--Spain
July 18: Anniversary of the Revolution--Nicaragua
July 20: Independence Day--Columbia
July 21: National Day--Belgium
July 22: National Liberation Day--Poland
July 23: National Day--Egypt
July 24: Simon Bolivar's Birthday--Ecuador and Venezuela
July 25: St. James Day--Spain
July 26: Independence Day--Liberia
July 26: Independence Day--Maldives
July 27: National Holiday--Belarus
July 28: Independence Day--Peru
July 30: National Holiday--Vanuatu

171

International Holiday Dates

August

August:	Independence Day (first Monday)--Jamaica
August:	Bank Holiday (first Monday)--Fiji, Grenada, Guyana, Hong Kong, Ireland, and Malawi
August:	Discovery Day (first Monday)--Trinidad and Tobago
August 1:	Lammas Day--England
August 1:	National Day--Switzerland
August 3:	Independence Day--Niger
August 4:	Independence Day--Burkina Faso
August 6:	Independence Day--Boliva
August 9:	National Day--Singapore
August 10:	Independence Day--Ecuador
August 11:	Independence Day--Chad
August 13:	Independence Day--Central African Republic
August 14:	Independence Day--Pakistan
August 15:	Independence Day--India
August 15:	Independence Day--South Korea
August 15:	Assumption Day--Catholic countries
August 15:	National Day--Congo
August 16:	Independence Day--Dominican Republic
August 17:	Independence Day--Indonesia
August 17:	Independence Day--Gabon
August 20:	National Holiday--Hungary
August 23:	Liberation Day--Romania
August 24:	National Holiday--Ukraine
August 25:	Independence Day--Uruguay
August 31:	Independence Day--Trinidad and Tobago
August 31:	National Holiday--Kyrgyzstan
August 31:	Independence Day--Malaysia

International Holiday Dates

September

September: Rose of Tralee Festival--Ireland (date varies)
September 1: Revolution Day--Libya
September 1: National Holiday--Uzbekistan
September 2: Independence Day--Vietnam
September 3: Independence Day--Qatar
September 6: Somhlolo (Independence) Day--Swaziland
September 7: Independence Day--Brazil
September 9: National Liberation Day--Bulgaria
September 9: National Holiday--North Korea
September 12: National Holiday--Cape Verde
September 12: Popular Revolution Commemoration Day--Ethiopia
September 14: Battle of San Jacinto Day--Nicaragua
September 15: Independence Day--Guatemala
September 15: Respect for the Aged Day--Japan
September 15: Independence Day--El Salvador
September 15: Independence Day--Honduras
September 15: Independence Day--Nicaragua
September 16: Independence Day--Mexico
September 16: Independence Day--Papua New Guinea
September 18: Independence Day--Chile
September 18: Independence Day--Costa Rica
September 19: Independence Day--St. Kitts and Nevis
September 21: National Holiday--Armenia
September 21: National Holiday--Belize
September 22: Independence Day--Mali
September 23: National Holiday--Saudi Arabia
September 24: Independence Day--Guinea-Bissau
September 26: Proclamation of the Republic--Yeman Arab Republic
September 28: Confucius' Birthday--Taiwan
September 30: Botswana Day--Botswana

International Holiday Dates

October

October 1-2:	National Day--People's Republic of China
October 1:	Armed Forces Day--Korea
October 1:	Independence Day--Nigeria
October 1:	Independence Day--Cyprus
October 2:	Mahatma Gandhi's Birthday--India
October 2:	Independence Day--Guinea
October 3:	National Day--Federal Republic of Germany
October 3:	National Foundation Day--Korea
October 4:	National Holiday--Lesotho
October 5:	Republic Day--Portugal
October 9:	Korean Alphabet Day
October 9:	Independence Day--Uganda
October 10:	Founding of Republic of China--Taiwan
October 10:	Fiji Day--Fiji
October 12:	Columbus Day--Spain, North and South America
October 12:	National Holiday--Equatorial Guinea
October 19:	Ascension of Muhammad Day--Indonesia
October 20:	Revolution Day--Guatemala
October 20:	Kenyatta Day--Kenya
October 21:	Independence Day--Marshall Islands
October 21:	National Holiday--Somalia
October 24:	United Nations Day--all U.N. member nations
October 24:	Independence Day--Zambia
October 26:	National Holiday--Australia
October 26:	Angram Day--Nauru or Naoero (Pacific Island)
October 27:	Independence Day--St. Vincent and the Grenadines
October 27:	National Holiday--Turkmenistan
October 28:	Greek National Day--Greece
October 28:	National Holiday--Czechoslovakia
October 29:	Republic Day--Turkey

International Holiday Dates

November

November 1: All Saint's Day--Catholic holiday in many countries
November 1: Anniversary of the Revolution--Algeria
November 1: National Holiday--Antigua and Barbuda
November 2: All Soul's Day--Ecuador, El Salvador, Luxembourg, Macao, Mexico, San Marino, Uruguay, and Vatican City

November 3: Culture Day--Japan
November 3: Independence Day--Panama
November 3: National Independence Holiday--Dominica
November 3: Independence Day--Micronesia
November 4: National Unity Day--Italy
November 4: Constitution Day--Tonga
November 5: Guy Fawkes Day--Great Britan
November 7-8: October Revolution Day--Russia
November 11: Armistice Day--Belgium, French Guinea and Tahiti
November 11: Veteran's Day--France
November 11: Independence Day--Angola
November 11: Remembrance Day--Canada and Bermuda
November 12: Sun Yat-sen's Birthday--Taiwan
November 15: Proclamation of the Republic Day--Brazil
November 18: National Holiday--Latvia
November 18-19: National Days--Oman
November 18: Independence Day--Morocco
November 19: National Holiday--Monaco
November 20: Anniversary of the Revolution--Mexico
November 22: Independence Day--Lebanon
November 23: Kinro-Kansha-No-Hi (Labor Thanksgiving Day)--Japan
November 25: Independence Day--Suriname
November 28: Independence Day--Mauritania
November 29: Liberation Day--Albania
November 30: National Heroes' Day--Philippines
November 30: Independence Day--Barbados
November 30: National Holiday--Benin

175

International Holiday Dates

December

December 1:   National Holiday--Central African Republic
December 1:   National Holiday--Romania
December 2:   National Holiday--Laos (Lao People's Democratic Republic)
December 2:   National Holiday--United Arab Emirates
December 5:   Columbus' Discovery of Haiti
December 5:   King's Birthday--Thailand
December 6:   Independence Day--Finland
December 7:   Independence Day--Ivory Coast, Republic of Cote d'Ivoire
December 8:   Feast of the Immaculate Conception--Catholic countries
December 9:   Independence Day--Tanzania
December 10: Constitution Day--Thailand
December 10: Human Rights Day--U.N. member nations
December 12: Jamhuri Day--Kenya
December 16: National Holiday--Bahrain
December 16: Victory Day--Bangladesh
December 17: National Holiday--Bhutan
December 18: National Holiday--Niger
December 25: Christmas Day--Christian countries
December 26: St. Stephen's Day--Austria, Ireland, Italy,
              Liechtenstein, San Marino, and Switzerland
December 26: Boxing Day--Great Britan and Northern Ireland
December 28: National Day and King's Birthday--Nepal
December 31: New Year's Eve--worldwide
December 31: Omisoka (Grand Last Day)--Japan
December 31: Hogmanay Day--Scotland

Collect Your Own Holiday Info:

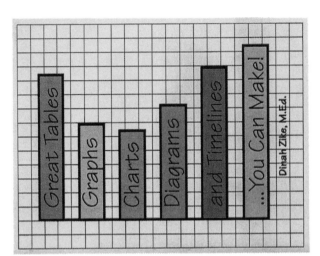

Dinah Zike's Big Book Of PROJECTS

How to design, develop, & make projects, from kindergarten through college

TEACHERS
STUDENTS
HOME SCHOOLING
CHURCHES
CLUBS AND ORGANIZATIONS

By Dinah Zike, M.Ed.

This 148-page book is the sequel to Dinah's *Big Book of Books and Activities*. It expands the use of manipulatives presented in *Big Book of Books and Activities*, and it introduces 14 folds not found in that book. The back section contains 64 duplicable pages of Dinah's publishing center graphics. **CCC91 $19.95**

Dinah Zike's Dinah-Might Activities Catalog

HOW TO USE Dinah Zike's *Big Book of Books*

In this lively, informative, 65-minute presentation, Dinah shows you how to get the most from your book! By Dinah Zike, M.Ed.

HOW TO USE Dinah Zike's *Big Book of Projects*

By Di...

Great Tables · Graphs · Charts · Diagrams · and Timelines · ...You Can Make!

Dinah Zike, M.Ed.

Standardized tests are filled with tables, graphs, charts, and diagrams. This "Dinah Zike book" presents easy-to-make teaching manipulatives and graphic organizers to teach your students these basic math life skills while preparing them for testing!! This 125-page book is multilevel. **CCC84 $19.95**

How-To Videos: In each of these one-hour videos, Dinah explains how to use her most popular books. The videos are appropriate for teachers and parents who have attended Dinah's seminars and need a review, or they serve as an introduction to those who have never seen Dinah Zike in person.

CCC85 *Video: How to Use Dinah Zike's Big Book of Books*
CCC86 *Video: How to Use Dinah Zike's Big Book of Projects* **$12.95 each.**

TO ORDER: Fax your orders to (210) 698-0095 Or call toll free 800-99-DINAH (993-4624)

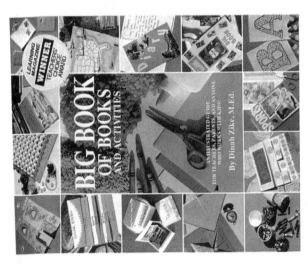

If you can afford only one of Dinah Zike's books, this is it! The award-winning *Big Book of Books and Activities* is used by thousands of teachers and parents internationally. Since its 1989 debut, it has become an education classic, and it is used by experienced teachers, student teachers, and home schooling parents alike. **CCC100 $19.95**

Dinah Zike's Big Book of Holiday Activities

A year-round guide to holiday fun based upon the folds and activities in Dinah Zike's award-winning *Big Book of Books & Activities*.

By Dinah Zike, M.Ed.

For years, teachers have encouraged Dinah to organize her manipulative holiday ideas into a book. *Big Book of Holiday Activities* contains 180 pages of monthly holiday activities and art patterns for the K-5 student. The book also contains lists of story starters, historic dates, and important birthdays to be used as holiday research and writing projects. **CCC83 $24.95**

educational publishing & consulting
p.o. box 690328
san antonio, texas 78269-0328 usa
office: (210) 698-0123
fax: (210) 698-0095
orders only: 1-800-99-dinah
e-mail: cecile@dinah.com
website: http://www.dinah.com

dma
dinah-might activities

ORDER FORM

Please fax your orders to (210) 698-0095
Or call toll free 800-99-DINAH (993-4624)

We accept

(CHECK ONE)

☐ Visa and
☐ Mastercard

Your Name _____

Address _____

City _____ State _____ Zip _____

Phone (___) _____ Fax (___) _____ E-mail _____

Purchase Order Number (If Needed) _____

If Using Purchase Order, Name & Address of School _____

NAME AS IT APPEARS ON CREDIT CARD _____

CREDIT CARD # _____ EXP. DATE _____

SIGNATURE _____

Item #	Qty.	Description	Each	Total
CCC 83		BIG BOOK OF HOLIDAY ACTIVITIES	$24.95	
CCC 84		GREAT TABLES, GRAPHS, CHARTS, DIAGRAMS, ETC. YOU CAN MAKE!	$19.95	
CCC 85		VIDEO: HOW TO USE THE BIG BOOK OF BOOKS	$12.95	
CCC 86		VIDEO: HOW TO USE THE BIG BOOK OF PROJECTS	$12.95	
CCC 87		TIME TWISTERS: THE LOST NAVIGATORS	$12.95	
CCC 88		TIME TWISTERS: THE HIDDEN CAVERNS	$12.95	
CCC 89		TIME TWISTERS: RAIN FOREST RESCUE	$12.95	
CCC 90		TIME TWISTERS: THE SEARCH FOR T. REX	$12.95	
CCC 91		BIG BOOK OF PROJECTS	$19.95	
CCC 92		THE EARTH SCIENCE BOOK	$12.95	
CCC 93		OLD TESTAMENT SUPPLEMENT TO BIG BOOK OF BOOKS $12.95		
CCC 94		NEW TESTAMENT SUPPLEMENT TO BIG BOOK OF BOOKS $12.95		
CCC 100		BIG BOOK OF BOOKS AND ACTIVITIES	$19.95	

Subtotal _____

Shipping & Handling _____

Sales Tax (Texas Residents 7.75%) _____

GRAND TOTAL _____

SHIPPING & HANDLING:
10% of total order or 8% of orders over $200.
$3.00 minimum S & H on all orders.
3-day, 2-day, & overnight UPS available. Call for prices.
Shipping outside of United States: Call for prices.

Please call for information on how
to book a Dinah Zike workshop
in your area.
(210) 698-0123

To receive a free catalog,
or to order other books
and materials by Dinah Zike,
please call
1-800-99DINAH

Visit our website at www.Dinah.com
E-mail us at dma@dinah.com